Rough Cuts

A Man, A Plan and A Gym

Uplifting Stories from the St. Louis 'Hood

Marshall Cohen

Copyright © 2013 by Marshall Cohen

ISBN: 978-1-891442-93-3

All rights reserved. No part of this book may be reproduced in any form or by any electronic or mechanical means, including information storage or retrieval systems, without permission in writing from the publisher, except by a reviewer, who may quote brief passages in review.

Editors: Richard H. Weiss, Carol Wise
Cover illustrator: Cbabi Bayoc
Cover design: Diann Cage Design Co.
Interior layout design: Emily Smith Design

Printed in the United States of America

To all the kids who want fishing rods so that they can fish.

To the donors and "investors" in Lift For Life Gym and Lift For Life Academy who helped sustain a safe place for children to grow, learn and be successful.

*To my parents, June and Julius Cohen,
who never gave up on me.*

To my sisters, Rosemary and Paula, who always believed in me.

To my wife Carla, who fell in love with Lift For Life before she fell in love with me, for sharing her non-profit expertise and driving me crazy with her editing help.

In memory of Gym members Vernon Russell and Terry Moore, and board member John Mann: my boys in the 'hood.

Table of Contents

Prologue	7
1. Comrade Winstein	11
2. "Mrs. Cohen, There Is Something Wrong with Marshall"	13
3. Oh Father, Where Art Thou?	17
4. Globe Drug — The Store for Social Services	19
5. The Incredible Mr. Dutton	24
6. The Victim and a $20-Bill	27
7. The Man with the Midas Touch	33
8. Dancing with Death	38
9. Marketing 101	41
10. Kol Nidre	47
11. Marathon Man	56
12. Twizzlers	61
13. My Friend Tommy	63
14. Heroes	66
15. Tonka Toys	71
16. Vernon	75
17. If the Shoe Fits	80
18. Guys & Dolls	85
19. A Diamond in the Rough	89
20. Chain Reaction	97
21. Roger That	101

22. It's a Small, Small World	107
23. Bien Sabrosa: The Taco Party	111
24. La Masquerade	114
25. Genuine	121
26. Innocent Giant	127
27. The Verbal Eviction	131
28. What Were You Doing When You Were Nine Years Old?	136
29. The Tale of Two Cars	140
30. The General Cometh	150
31. What Comes Around, Goes Around	154
32. Mein Kinder	160
33. Do it Now, Because You Can't Do Anything When You Are Dead	171

What's Happening Now	180

About the Author	181

Prologue

On a spring morning in the early 1990s, I climbed the steep, metal stairs to my dad's discount store, Globe Drug, on the second floor of a downtown warehouse building. I grabbed a quick breath as I stepped into the retail area lit by a multitude of fluorescent lights, hanging willy-nilly from the cracked ceiling. Walking over to the counter that served as my desk, I pondered the dreary tasks of the day: stocking shelves with discount soap powder, waiting on customers as indecisive as chess players in an endless game, and making sure fools attempting a brief high wouldn't help themselves to the Mogen David we sold for a buck.

When you work in a space for 20-plus years, you get used to its digestive rumbles and rattles. But that morning I heard something strange coming from the stairs above me. The staircase led to a handball court and office suite – relics from when the building housed one of the largest shoe distribution centers in the Midwest, Endicott Johnson Shoe Company. Had March winds brought an extra shake or two to the door? There it was again. I decided to check it out.

As I climbed the short flight of curved, tin stairs, the sounds changed from clanks and clinks to soft whimpers and muffled cries. Soon a body came into focus, hunched over and shaking, like an ice skater just pulled

Globe Drug warehouse store located in downtown St. Louis.
Photo by Laura Thake.

from a semi-frozen pond.

It was Vernon Russell, then 15 years old. Was this the same sweet kid that I remembered? The one who beamed with pride ….who used to wear his weightlifting medals for days after a contest? Was this the kid…

"It's me, man, quiet! The police are looking for me!" Blood started to stream from Vernon's lip mixing with the tears streaming down his face.

"Vernon, what happened?" I whispered, so the customers below wouldn't hear us.

"Nothing," he lied, as more tears flowed and his knees shook.

"Are you okay?"

He sniffed a couple of times while wiping his face with his blood-stained, ripped shirt that had been white a day ago. I waited. After working with both customers and kids for years, I had learned not to push. The beans would spill when they were good and ready.

"Me and this dude stole this car in Illinois. Cops started chasing us so we drove it across the river," he choked out through his tears. "We hit a car and he couldn't get out. They arrested him. I just took off."

Vernon leaned up and peered over the stairway, checking to see if he was being followed.

"Please don't tell anyone!" he begged.

"Oh, Vernon!" I said finally, as I shook my head. "I won't."

Checking to see if the coast was clear, Vernon limped back down the stairs. "I'll be okay," he said with a shake in his voice and a wave of his hand.

I watched him sneak out the back door and slip down the steep metal staircase to the garage below.

At the time, I thought this brush with the law would scare him back to school, back to the gym, back to his happy-go-lucky ways. But years later, I am ashamed at my complete cluelessness. I should have called the police.

Although I was his coach, Vernon taught me more than I could ever teach him. And, in the end, I failed him. All I can do now is tell his story. And the stories of other kids.

The last thing anyone would expect from me – or that I would expect from myself – is a book. As you will read, I have been called many things over my span of 50 years. But "author" was never one of them.

Of course, until about 25 years ago, I never expected to have a story to tell. I was the son of a middle-class Jewish merchant who ran a discount store in downtown St. Louis. My mom and dad raised three children in the burbs. I was a lousy student with a mind that wandered here, there and everywhere. For a short time, I had a brief marriage to alcohol and marijuana. I dealt with depression and despair.

In between, I worked at the store and could have done that for the rest of my life, ordering cigarettes, candy, beer and wine, overstock shoes and clothing …. stocking shelves … ringing up sales… keeping the books … and doing it all over again, month after month. Though it seemed mundane, it was an honorable way to make a living.

We offered something for everyone: bargains for the downtown professional, cheap booze for those in need of a daytime high, and staples for neighborhood families.

My favorite customers were the kids from the nearby projects. As a group, these are the kids who commit more crimes, spend more time in prison, require more social services and, in general, scare the hell out of many of us. But I wasn't selling candy and soda to statistics. The kids who walked into Globe Drug were full of energy and bursting with potential, even if some of them were doing a bit of shoplifting.

I noticed that running the streets was considered an acceptable "after-school activity". Unlike kids in the county, inner city children in St. Louis have few safe options after school.

So one day I decided to open a gym and invite kids from the neighborhood to join.

Just like that.

As a kid, lifting weights had boosted my confidence and given me something positive to do. Maybe it would give these kids something positive too.

I had no business plan. I didn't know a 501(c)(3) from a 401(k). I winged it, just like the kids in the neighborhood have to do when their mothers are unable to put food on the table or get them to school.

Still my instincts told me on that spring day in 1988 that I was making a sound investment because I can do simple math.

Annual cost to incarcerate a felon: $25,000 vs. stocking a rundown warehouse with weight and fitness equipment: $10,000.

I called the gym Lift For Life. How it got that name is a story in itself, which is included in this book. It succeeded way beyond my dreams and that of just about every boy and girl who walked through the door, grabbed a barbell and started lifting.

Rough Cuts will take you from my own somewhat privileged childhood into the childhood of others less fortunate. You will meet kids like Neil who worked his way out of the 'hood one lift at a time. And kids like

Vernon who couldn't overcome the lousy hand he was dealt.

In most cases, I have used the first and last names of the people I've encountered over the years. They are real. In some cases, I have used just first names to protect their identities.

I hope these stories inspire you.

Do the math.

That's all I ask.

Marshall Cohen
February, 2013

Training with his buddies at Lift For Life Gym kept Vernon (middle) off the streets – for a while.

I

Comrade Winstein

For 20 years, Mr. Winstein parked his car in front of his suburban ranch in exactly the same spot. That's just the kind of guy he was. I know this because, night after night, I watched him pull up in his well-maintained Chevy sedan. That's just the kind of kid I was.

With a quarter-inch crew cut crowning his round head, Mr. Winstein resembled Nikita Khrushchev, the temperamental Soviet leader from the 1950s and '60s, and in more ways than one. He tolerated the neighborhood kids with an aloof attitude and even allowed our spirited games of Red Rover, Red Rover to spill over into his manicured lawn. But it was clear he didn't like it.

Truth be told, I didn't much care for the backyard game myself, although you couldn't tell by the way I sped across the lawn and slammed my skinny six-year-old body against the arms of the older kids. Again and again. There oughta be a law.

As the sun set on a warm autumn day, Mr. Winstein hobbled over to our game. Were we in trouble? He verbally corralled us around his front steps to rattle his sabers.

"See this caulk? Do not touch it," he barked. Mr. Winstein had just laid caulk around his picture window. Pointing at the smooth white lines, he repeated his warning, "This caulk is still wet. Do not touch it!"

Everyone solemnly nodded then quickly darted back to the game. Well, almost everyone.

Gummy. White. Softness.

Transfixed by the creamy smoothness before me, a strange stillness came over me as I pressed my index and middle fingers into the soft stuff. My fingers sank deep into the forbidden goo that surrounded Mr. Winstein's window. I stared ahead, floating in a sea of new found tranquility. Until I noticed someone staring back at me. INCOMING!

Mr. Winstein bolted from his Lazy Boy. "Marshall!" Reverse engines. Sprinting from my imaginary starting blocks, I raced home to safety, never looking back.

I learned two things that day. One, I could run as fast as the dickens. Especially with a World War II vet with a slight giddyup in his step hard on my tail. Second, there was definitely something wrong with me. I couldn't follow instructions. Maybe that's just the kind of kid I was.

My Bar Mitzvah, 1973.

2

"Mrs. Cohen, There Is Something Wrong With Marshall"

My poor mother, what could she do? I was her middle child, bracketed by two sisters, but was easily twice as much trouble.

At home, I would bring a hose running with water into the kitchen to show her that I had just watered the garden. At school, I daydreamed and was out of focus with even the smallest tasks. If the assignment didn't "turn me on," I entered a different place, a different time. We were given frequent assessment tests, the kind that need a #2 pencil to fill in the oval. To me, they became a game. After one question and its guessed-at answer, I would haphazardly color in the ovals in no particular order and without reading anything, just to be the second or third one finished in the class. Anything to beat Mary Becht or Judy Krauss. I didn't try to finish first, because that would have been too obvious to the teacher and would have given my antics away.

After the test results came back, and my mother was summoned to school once again for the ominous parent–teacher

Mom, Dad, sisters Paula (left) and Rosemary share the frame with my blonde afro, 1976.

conference, she was told of a severe deficiency in my learning, as they put it. Back then there was no diagnosis for anything, either you were "normal and functioning," or not.

At one conference, I remember one of my grade school teachers saying, "Mrs. Cohen, there is something wrong with Marshall." That comment hurt me for the first 20 or so years of my life, until I understood that all kids, regardless of what is inside their skulls, are special. To this day, I have used that meeting to remind me that each of us is unique.

THE AMAZING ADVENTURES OF THE D-MINUS BOY

Because I was failing in school, I earned the illustrious label from several neighborhood kids, "D-Minus Boy." There were many days when our group of neighborhood kids would all play together, and I would be greeted by, "There's D-Minus Boy" and worse.

I realized even then that my school was promoting me to the next grade to get me through the system and out the door. Being called "D-Minus Boy" was tough, but with the resilience of childhood, I blocked it out.

My mom hired tutors and tried bribing me to do homework with things like Batman cutouts. Didn't work.

I could never sit still in class, always fidgeting and wiggling like a leaf on a tree. Even at the afternoon Orthodox Hebrew School I attended in first grade, the teacher told me 'sit down or you can just leave!' The next thing I remember was seeing my mother driving along McKnight road passing me as I was walking home. What I'd pay to have seen her face. Furious as she was, what kind of teacher tells a student that he can leave?

Meanwhile, no one observed the many things that were clicking in my brain like a haywire fax machine spitting out a twenty-two page misprint document with a thick, juicy black line running down center court.

I don't know if it was my infatuation with how things worked, or the mercury poisoning I probably acquired from breaking open glass thermometers that my parents got as promotional items from insurance peddlers. I liked watching how the silvery stuff would flow on the basement floor with my pencil leading the trail. I adored putting together plastic models and didn't even need to look at the directions. I'm sure the glue was toxic, but after going through many models and inhaling tubes and tubes of glue while assembling them, I still retained some brain function.

One of my greatest joys was when my dad occasionally brought home an empty bathroom tissue case filled with damaged toys or ones that were missing pieces. There was no rhyme or reason to anything in the box, but to me, putting things together and fixing them was one of the most rewarding experiences imaginable. The old Creepy Crawler bug-making machines would be banned in today's world, but they were stupendous. You could get third-degree burns on your fingers and wrists from pulling out the hot metal plate. At the same, though, you could melt other toys and what-nots scattered throughout the house that no one would ever remember missing.

With my parents busy working in the family store, my childhood passed relatively unsupervised. My experiments continued, culminating in the days after a Fourth of July with a rocket's red glare.

It started just after the Fourth when I went on my annual scavenger hunt, collecting faulty bottle rockets, cones, and other firecrackers that the neighbors had left to clean up the next day. I had a skill set in defective Chinese fireworks and had extracted the gunpowder to build rockets and bombs. The rocket I built was was slightly crooked, but it looked cool. I was very proud that I hadn't needed to buy anything to make this contraption fly. Empty cardboard tubes from paper towel and toilet paper rolls worked very well, or so I thought until the rocket arced and landed atop a neighbor's roof, the Wymans, 500 meters away. I turned into a pathetic criminal, dashing to our house for "cover." Did I really think the police wouldn't figure out where the rocket had come from?

Instead of going to their house, knocking on their door, and saying something like, "Excuse me, Mrs. Wyman, I'm sorry to bother you. I'm not selling any of my dad's overproduced produce today, but thanks for your past support. It sure is sunny today, isn't it? By the way, I just launched a rocket that was supposed to land across the street in the school playground but happened to misfire and wedge itself between your gutter and a shingle, kind of near your patio in the back. Oh, and the gunpowder engine is still firing its afterburner stage. Do you mind if I bring over a ladder and retrieve it?"

Fortunately, the rocket burned itself out without the Wymans ever knowing how close their house came to burning up.

On another occasion, I rewired a cassette tape recorder and plugged it back in the wall, only to notice after the black puff of smoke dissipated, that I had lost my eyebrows and acquired singed eyelashes.

I would play chess constantly after a neighborhood kid taught me how to play. Oftentimes without an opponent, I'd play myself by turning the board back and forth. I bought foreign language cassette programs to teach myself the languages.

My pyromania extended to holding small bonfires in old tin Maxwell House coffee cans. They were great on cold, chilly days. My friend and I built a small clubhouse that looked like a shanty in a Soweto township. Ventilation was nonexistent, and when we fired up the coffee can with twigs, newspaper scraps, and assorted dried leaves, it warmed the structure nicely.

However, we decided to take it a step further. I had taken a handful of tear-gas pellets from my dad's store. Since dad had no intention of selling them, I figured I could help myself like taking a scoop of assorted gumdrops. On this particular dreary afternoon, a couple of pellets were resting comfortably in my pocket when I decided to drop them into the flaming can. I particularly liked the dinging sound the pellets made as they hit the tin bottom. For a couple of minutes, my friend and I continued our discussion of the usual kid stuff when we were surprised by a loud pop emanating from the can.

In my life I have had the dubious pleasure of getting kicked in the groin, spat upon, and landing forcefully on my adolescent package while doing jumps on my bike, but those are only minor bumps in a young boy's life.

There is nothing, and let me repeat, nothing, that compares to being in a three by four foot clubhouse and zero ventilation when a couple of virgin tear gas pellets explode. As the tear gas permeated our nasal passages and eyes, we burst out of the clubhouse, rolling on the autumn ground, crying and holding our hands pressed firmly against our eyes as the pain came in increments of painful and fucking painful.

So back in the day, when Peter Jennings was on the evening news talking about the latest protest in sunny Romania or the latest upheaval in Idi Amin's quaint city of Kampala, I had a deeper appreciation, a closer relationship, to what protesters go through as police shoot tear gas over their freedom-aspiring heads.

Mischief in the kitchen.

3

Oh Father, Where Art Thou?

I grew up with a workaholic parent and it was difficult. It seemed like my father, Julius, worked at his store more hours than there were in a week.

While I didn't comprehend it until we grew up, my sisters and I had a unique relationship with our father. My father was tall, thin and good looking. He once told me: "In the army, everyone in my platoon would follow me at R&R because I knew how to get the women."

He was a quiet man and rarely spoke to his kids. I didn't realize how odd it was until I was 12 and the two of us went out to dinner together when my mom and sisters were out of town. I felt very uncomfortable having a conversation with him at the restaurant table. He tried to talk to me, but with the absence of a close relationship up to that point, the conversation was meaningless. It was not until I started working for him full time that we grew close and the relationship that I dreamed of was finally fulfilled.

Most of our Sundays were different. Instead of the standard trips to the zoo, shooting hoops or playing catch, we were encouraged to plant, rake, and saw tree limbs. I was like the kid in the Karate Kid movie, put through the interminable paces of shining a car — "wax on wax off." Sometimes I resented it, but after a while I realized I had rounded into good shape thanks to all this hard work.

On the first day of softball practice, some of the kids made fun of me. When it was my turn up at the plate, I held the bat with a crisscross grip as my father had never taught me the proper approach. The gym teacher gave me this I can't believe it look and said, "Don't you know how to hold the bat?" I was speechless. The only reasonable response was no…not really, but I do know how to make half-sour kosher pickles from the cucumbers we grew.

My dad would load up a wagon with fresh-grown produce from his backyard garden and tell me to sell it to the neighbors. At first, I was nervous ringing doorbells and wondering whether the neighbors would run me off their front lawn with a wagon full of vegetables. But every house bought something, either because my parents bought candy from their kids over the years and they felt the need to reciprocate, or they actually wanted some delicious, ripe, homegrown tomatoes. To me, it had nothing to do with making money, just the action and adrenaline rush that came with each sale. It gave me confidence that I lacked.

It's interesting what we self select to remember and how those memories play a role our lives. One evening while walking into a pizzeria, our family encountered a somewhat disheveled Vietnam veteran with missing limbs sitting on the floor in a narrow hallway with his crutches beside him. Seeing him made me uncomfortable. But as we passed, dad handed him some money. At first the man refused to take it, but dad insisted and after a few uncomfortable seconds, the vet accepted the temporary relief. Although I sometimes resented dad for not being available, he gave me his gift of giving to others without expecting anything in return.

Dad's favorite perch – behind the liquor counter at Globe, 1971.

4

Globe Drug – The Store For Social Services

I was a product of the farmer mentality whether I liked it or not. Back in the old days, a farmer would have a lot of kids who were expected to work on the farm. In my family, this meant that instead of attending school football games or other festivities on Saturdays, my parents expected me to help out at the family discount store. Looking back, even though I missed seeing cheerleaders do splits, I learned life lessons from the host of people who shopped at the store, and particularly the employees themselves.

The store was called Globe Drug. My father and uncles opened for business just before the end of World War II. Their philosophy was simple: Buy it damn cheap and sell it cheaper than the competitor's store down the street.

They were well ahead of Sam Walton. Globe carried a large inventory with bargains jammed all over the store as haphazard as a three-year-old's finger painting.

Customers would come from near and far to buy masses of over-produced items: Halloween mellowcreme pumpkins the day after Halloween, ladies bowling shoes going two pairs for a buck, men's size 55w maroon polyester pants, 55-cent pints of Mogen David apple wine that hadn't made the Kosher cut, Easter lilies blooming too early or too late for the Easter holiday. You name it, Globe had it.

I just couldn't comprehend some of the things my uncles bought. To top off all the unimaginable things was the trailer-load of fallout shelter containers. They were loaded with toilet tissue, feminine napkins, bandages, and included a cardboard toilet seat to put on top of the round container to use as a toilet. Now who in their right mind would think they could sell them other than my uncles and father? I never knew what they paid for them, but when they started to sell off the toilet tissue and other contents piece by piece, my state of mind changed from "are you kidding me, you bought these?" to "you guys are geniuses!"

I was terrible at math in school, but at the store, it was a different story. One day I figured out that if you put a dollar sign in front of numbers, they made a lot more sense. I didn't need to know about Pythagorean's theorem. To make a sale, I could add, subtract, and hustle numbers in the blink of an eye.

Back then I would chuckle at some of the things my Uncle Louis would buy and wonder what he was thinking — like the size 55-waist pants. But I learned my lesson when word got out in town that we had extra-plus-sized pants, cuffed at that. Dozens of portly men came in to buy six pairs at a time for $4.99.

Then there was the holiday candy. We would buy truckload after truckload after a holiday, cleaning out the candy factories. But my uncles and father had a way to move it, not only by putting it in cold storage for the next year, but by making a grocers' mix out of it and selling it faster than a three-stack-pancake breakfast at IHOP. Whatever they bought, whatever it happened to be, they had the gift of turning someone else's leftovers into a profit.

Globe Drug also built its business on liquor and beer. Regular customers would call in orders and we would fill them ahead of time, so they didn't have to wait around. At that time Old Style, Stag, and Olympia ruled the kingdom of discount beer, unlike today's sexy craft beer market.

You could walk into the warehouse and see multiple pallets of beer that could be bought for next to nothing. There was even a time that we had Billy Beer from Jimmy Carter's brother. I think it sold for $2.99 a case. Do the math: 13 cents a can. We had a lot of can collectors come in just to corner the market. I'm sure they didn't make jack.

Some of the liquors were amazing as well as intoxicating, especially to a 13-year-old. I'm surprised I didn't start drinking sooner. I particularly remember "Voodoo Juice," the product supposedly of a Haitian voodoo doctor that had sediments of fruit pulp floating at the bottom when you held it up to the light. Then there was the multitude of wines – finds of a lifetime for a buck ninety-nine. Doctors and wine connoisseurs would come on the chance they would find a $100 bottle of rare Merlot or Cabernet. Some would buy a bottle, go back to their Jaguar or Mercedes Benz in the parking lot, pull out a cork opener and wine glass and sample it. If it passed muster, they would rush back to buy as much of the inventory as they could.

Our clientele was as eclectic as the merchandise. Amish from the back-country buying damaged or ripped sacks of sugar for making jams and jellies; men who made their living at auctions and flea markets, peddling whatever the deal of the week was; mothers of ten trying to buy enough food to last the month, while futilely struggling to keep their kids corralled in the checkout line; winos in search of cheap wine to get them through another miserable day; renowned doctors seeking expensive Merlot at an inexpensive price; and an occasional thief, attempting to slip what he could down his pants or into the folded shopping bag he happened to bring along.

Our family store was like a must-see sitcom. You couldn't invent a cast of characters like that. Well, maybe Tarantino or the Coen brothers could approximate it.

Yet in this sitcom, I could step outside my sheltered Jewish suburban life. Before I officially started working at the age of 12, I thought everyone got three meals a day, could walk out of their house without being shot, raped, or assaulted, and slept in a comfortable bed.

It took me several decades to realize that, although the family store operated as a business, it was in a sense a cover for a 501(c)(3), a clandestine charity operation. My family had a weakness for the desperate and desolate. I can't tell you how many times my relatives would tell a hungry shopper to "pay me for it later," knowing they might never see the money. Although my father and uncles tried at every turn to make money, they were equally always helping people on some level. They just had that Mitzvah touch.

My uncles and dad would always hire the latest trend in immigrants. Whenever there was a conflict in the world visible on the nightly news, shortly after my family would hire several arriving refugees from those locations, regardless of their English skills. They tended to work at the store for a year or two, and then they moved on. Although I invariably got Ds and Fs in social studies, this was a real life lesson and it registered deeply.

When the Vietnam War came to a close, we hired several Vietnamese to fill Christmas stockings and Easter baskets. I became very close to them, not only because I wanted to be supportive, but because I was intrigued with the stories they shared. Maybe I related to them because of the immigrant experience of my grandparents, or maybe I was just appalled at how much people could harm one another. All of the Vietnamese working for us had lost a family member in the conflict.

In the early '80s my family hired an assortment of South American refugees coming from ever-changing political climates. I heard stories from those workers about having to choose between factions.

When Fidel Castro permitted a brief exodus of Cubans in the Mariel boatlift in 1980, including some from his prisons, we hired at least a dozen. Most were great people, and I am friends with them to this day, but others were violent criminals and we inherited that problem.

When Ethiopia went through a political crisis, and our country allowed many to resettle, we hired Solomon, who claimed to be a hybrid Jew. He was a former university professor but didn't seem to mind that he was reduced to sweeping floors and putting out stock.

I learned some foreign tongues as a result of these encounters. I enjoyed learning Vietnamese and I paid one of the workers to teach me how to speak after work. The employee brought some short books to help me learn. I was stunned when one of the books contained phrases like: "Are there any weapons in your village?" or "When were the Viet Cong here last?" It turned out the phrases came from a military field manual.

Family members also worked at Globe Drug. My Aunt Rose in particular, all of 87 pounds, was a fascinating person. She had the God-given knack for being able to sell anything regardless of the season. She could sell leftover Halloween candy during the height of the Christmas or Easter season, talking a customer into buying a solid chocolate bunny with a broken ear or two.

Even though she was small and frail, word on the street was "You better not mess with Rose." Occasionally, one of our regular wine connoisseurs would slide an unpaid item down his pants. Aunt Rose would confront him in an operatic voice demanding "Take that out of your pants." He would do so, apologize profusely and comply with Aunt Rose's instructions to atone for the crime by moving boxes around for an upcoming seasonal display.

Other workers became like family to me.

Around the time I was thirteen and working every Saturday and then some, I met Joe, the new "porter." A neat, lanky fellow in his 60s or 70s, he was always friendly to me, perhaps because I was the boss' son, or simply because he was just a good guy.

Over the course of several Saturdays, we began engaging in workplace dialogues, the sort that takes place between tasks, a comment or two before turning around to go back to stocking shelves, carrying out paid orders, or mopping up a busted jar of sweet dill slices. He told me he used to work on the railroad as a porter and made good money. But as freight trucks became a primary mode of transport, the rail car industry declined. He found himself suddenly out of the only job he had held in his whole adult life. I don't think he had a pension. I had the feeling from my conversations with him that he had been rooked out of a pension.

One of Joe's jobs was to fill the beer orders, but it became quickly apparent that he always made mistakes. Whenever the orders were checked, they always had to be corrected and refilled. At first, Dad or his assistant manager would help fix the order, but the situation only worsened. A simple order that should have taken a few minutes would instead take twenty or thirty and still be incorrect.

Then came the whispering, circulating through the store's rumor mill like a wobbly ceiling fan. "Joe can't read! He's dumb; he can't fill an order." When I heard these rumors I couldn't believe that anyone born in this country couldn't read, especially a man in his 60s. I found it mean-spirited and disrespectful that others were making fun of him, like a broken toy. It especially bothered me because Joe was becoming my friend, someone I looked up to.

So I decided to investigate. The next time Joe was working on a beer order, I told him I would help. He would read the order and I would fetch the beer. He held the order several inches from his eyes, trying mentally to reach for something, but all that came was a moment of silence that wracked me with shame.

He quickly passed the paper to me and said, with downcast eyes, "Point to the beer and I'll get it."

What does a 13-year-old kid say to an adult he has just embarrassed?

How can this happen in America? Was it because he was one of the old school African Americans who got the short end of the stick some 60 years ago?

Though my dad knew of this "disability," he kept Joe working at the store. When possible, I always made an effort to help Joe with the beer orders. I arranged to have him take certain carry outs, knowing which customers gave tips and which ones didn't. I didn't mind giving up the chump change knowing full well that to Joe, every nickel counted.

This youthful experience with my friend, Joe, was the first in a series of consciousness raising episodes that would lead me down a different path.

5

The Incredible Mr. Dutton

I eventually made it out of grade school and into junior high. Nothing much had changed, so I was herded with the rest of the "dumb" kids in a class that traveled together for two years. I called it the "cell block" of the dummy kids. I don't know whose idea it was that if we were all together, we would learn something, let alone be taught at the same level. To think that the Ladue school system, one of the richest districts in the state of Missouri, could have 25 or so challenged kids in one classroom with one teacher and not pack in extra staff and backup to help was mind-boggling. Our group also wasn't so dumb that we didn't notice why we had been segregated.

If anything was honed in that class, it was my skill at making everyone laugh. The classroom was my platform for improv-comedy shows. I wasn't the only entertainer in these shows, but I became so proficient I knew when to deliver the laugh and when to let up. I learned to back off when the teacher's face started to flush carnation pink, before she could call me out. I was smart enough to stay out of detention.

In some classes, there always seemed to be an assigned novel or other work of fiction that was required reading. I don't think I read any of those novels, and, in fact, doubt that throughout my entire secondary school career I read any book from beginning to end. It was only after I graduated that I realized I had a serious reading problem. It wasn't that I couldn't read; it was my lack of focus. The teachers just mistook it for not doing the work. They failed to comprehend that when I started to read my mind would drift to a different planet.

That changed when Mr. Dutton, my eighth grade social studies teacher, announced the assignment that would finally catch my attention. He told us to write a paper about a group of kids stranded on a deserted island. In writing the story, we had to use objects like coconuts, rocks, whatever you could find on the island, to survive and lead the group to well-being. Well, there it was. The light bulb in the strand of Christmas lights lit back up. For the next four days I pounded my Mom's dull-yellow typewriter with misspelled words, errant punctuation, and a story as Mr. Dutton put it, that was, "The best thing I have ever read for the past 20 years!"

He made that proclamation in front of the entire class as he held up my paper. I couldn't have been more proud until I noticed the large "F" marked thickly in red magic marker. Mr. Dutton said that there was no way that I wrote the story and asked me point blank, who wrote it for me?

Perhaps he had cause for suspicion. I had never gotten more than a D-plus for a half a year in his class. The bell rang as I tried to plead my case. Mr. Dutton refused to listen. I left the classroom and went to the nearest trash bin to throw my story away.

For the next several years, I wrote very little.

TWO PEAS IN A POD

Mr. Dutton wasn't the only sub-standard teacher that I encountered. In gym class we were blessed with two of the most abusive PE teachers imaginable. They ran their class as though we were in the first days of boot-camp training for the Vietnam War. Worse, our district had come up with the bizarre idea of sending all the seventh grade students into PE class at one time with three teachers to supervise the circus. I'm sure the rationale was to give the other "core" teachers a planning period without having to hire more staff.

Two of the coaches echoed the characters Thing One and Thing Two from the Dr. Suess book the *Cat in the Hat*. They would yell either loud or louder to get students to comply. Humiliation, fear, and complete disrespect were the tools they believed necessary for a good ass kickin' physical education. Students were routinely called out because they made a mistake or didn't move fast enough.

To keep order among such a large number of students, they assigned drill upon drill. These would, presumably, perfect us. During basketball season, we did the usual wind sprints. You remember those — you have to bend down and touch a line, then run back to the other side of the court, touch the other line. We repeated the cycle until we were drenched in sweat. We also fine-tuned our passing, dribbling, and other elements of the game.

Then it was time to learn how to pivot. You simply plant one foot like a eucalyptus tree in the mountains of Malaysia, and move your other foot while swinging your body around. Pretty simple, right? They had us line up in rows, and then they shouted out, "Left," and we rotated left; and then, "Right," and so forth. The only problem was, I didn't happen to know my left foot from my right. Or maybe I was just nervous.

I don't quite remember how it happened, but Thing One and Thing Two decided to make examples out of the ones who were rotating the wrong way. Of course I was the fortunate one to be pulled out in front of my classmates.

At first they told everyone to stop and had me do it solo. They barked, "Right" or "Left," and, of course, given this unannounced audition in front of my entire class, I went in completely the wrong direction. The class broke out in laughter watching me twist the wrong way each time. Thing One's face turned beet red in anger. Thing Two had a silly grin on his face, the same one that he wore when he flirted with the ninth grade cheerleaders. After I kept making errors, they asked me to hold up my left hand and then my right, and I either didn't hold up the correct one or I was too withdrawn even to try.

As my classmates laughed, Thing One and Thing Two finally gave up on me, and the nightmare class came to an end. After we got dressed, several classmates approached me in the hall and apologized for the way I had been treated, telling me not to worry about it. I was flattered and pleased that they had the maturity even at 13 years old to know that this display had been completely disrespectful and counterproductive. Who were the real adults?

There is one thing that is just plain common sense: teaching is best done not through intimidation, humiliation, and anger, but through respect and encouragement.

6

The Victim and a $20 Bill

I liked swimming a heck of a lot. We belonged to the Jewish Community Center, and my mom would take us there almost every day as a social activity. But in my pre-pubescent years leading up to my bar mitzvah, I got socialized in an inappropriate way.

Today the media puts everything out there for discussion. Nothing is taboo. But when I was growing up, some things just didn't surface and no one talked about them. In school they pushed us to learn math and reading. No one ever discussed inappropriate touching. So when it happened, we didn't have the tools, the mental plan to talk about it or deal with it, but there is no doubt that it changed us.

The Jewish Community Center pool was a busy, crowded place. Day camps and other recreational groups used the same pool. You needed at least a professional football team roster to have enough guards for all the shifts.

That summer they had just built a senior complex on the campus. It was a nice place, built primarily to provide for seniors on a fixed income safe living quarters with a Jewish lifestyle and kosher meals. Of course, one of the amenities was open access to the JCCA facility, including the swimming pool.

Who would think for a moment that a retired senior would do anything to harm kids? But on one occasion, one of the seniors was hanging out in, as the kids called it, the "four-foot" section. At first he just splashed the kids and smiled a lot. Then he started to throw kids in the water. But alas, little by little, as kids started swimming to him to be thrown in the air, and his "fun magnet" was working full throttle, he started sticking his hands down swim trunks and swimsuits alike. Now most kids after getting touched perhaps thought "well his hand must have slipped" and didn't think much of it and swam away. Then he began to get more aggressive, since his appetite had been whetted. He started pursuing some kids and continued his antics.

I, too, had been the recipient of some of his hand movements, and again, was so surprised at the unwelcome visitor to my backside that I just didn't know what to do. With this particular man, it wasn't just young boys — but girls were in the mix, too. In this engagement, there was no prejudice. And that may have been his downfall.

Eventually, his disappearing-hand tricks fell on the wrong kid and she stormed out of the pool and told her mother. Word spread quickly as the mother went to talk to the manager to get this freak out of the pool. As word circulated among the sunbathing mothers, my mother asked me if he had touched me. Then she, too, joined the procession to complain to the pool manager.

At first the manager maintained that he was just an old man and that he couldn't throw him out of the pool. It was his right to be here, too. Most importantly, the manager said, "No, he would never do that to anyone!"

The girl's mother was not persuaded. The exchange went on for several 10- and 20-minute sessions, with her storming off and then returning for another round. Finally, the pool manager pulled the plug on the man's antics and told him to leave.

In today's world, the mother would have called the police. The interesting thing about this is that no one talked about it after it happened. No one was trained to tell you that freaks aren't supposed to do things like that. So it just sits there inside your brain and festers.

I later learned that predators come in all ages. My best friend and I loved to go to the evening sports camp that our school district hosted. The program offered everything from shooting hoops to baseball, and yes, free swim. While my friend and I were focused on playing and having fun, there was a predator there who was focused on scoping us out. Who would ever have thought about that in a public pool with an adult lifeguard on duty?

An older teen grabbed me from behind, and I tried to wrestle away. I thought he was just going to dunk me, which is what often happened with bigger, stronger kids. Instead, he pulled me to the deep end so I couldn't stand up, he then settled into a position from behind, while he had his arms wrapped around my arms and torso. And then it started. I was so surprised that I just didn't know what to do.

While he started his humping maneuvers against my discount swim trunks, I continued to fight him off, but to little avail. My friend didn't quite know what was happening, and it's not something a kid, say 12 or 13 years old, would yell out to the lifeguard, or for that matter anyone else in the pool. "Umm…excuse me…., sorry to bother you, but would you mind telling this guy latched around me like a salamander mating in the treetops TO GET OFF ME?"

Eventually, he let go, and then immediately grabbed my friend, who was in striking distance. I saw him struggle too. But I was in such dismay, such disillusionment, that I couldn't function. He continued the same actions on my friend until he succeeded in pulling away from him.

We were both so embarrassed, so shocked, that we left the pool and quickly got dressed. No conversation took place, and we darted off to another activity. To this day we haven't talked about it.

Unfortunately, this wasn't the last of my encounters with aberrant behavior. Years later, I was in the locker room at school one day changing to go to practice. One of my teachers happened to be walking through the locker room and stopped to talk to me as I was changing clothes. I found it odd that previously he had never asked me questions about how my classes were going, yet he now found it appropriate to have a discussion while I was in my Fruit of the Loom skivvies.

Thankfully, nowadays, children are taught about inappropriate touching and things that are just not right; and adults can get their asses locked up for doing them. Even so, there are still plenty of victims. And I can testify that these pool crimes and other assaults leave scars that last a lifetime.

DUMBELLS

It's interesting how new paths open when others close. I can't say precisely when, but around the time the events happened at the pool and while I continued to be bullied at school, I found a path to a future.

One day, out of sheer boredom, I accompanied my mom and sisters on one of their long weekend shopping expeditions. I was strolling through the store like a ghost lost in a graveyard when I stumbled upon the sporting goods aisle.

As I strolled past baseball gloves and bats, fishing rods and hooks, and the latest polyester gym shorts, I turned a corner and there it was, sitting enticingly on the shelf in a stapled brown box with barely legible blue printing. The display showed a bar loaded with plastic weights and two dumbbells flanking each side. Some people find going to a casino to be the ultimate pleasure: the clanking bells, the bright lights, the chance to win money. For me the jackpot was one of those $19.95 weight sets.

The process in our family for getting something that you wanted was first to ask, knowing that you weren't going to get it. Then you begged weekly, here and there, to slowly work mom into at least considering it. When I first brought it up, my mom and dad immediately said no. They thought weights would cause hernias like the one my dad was carrying around in his pants.

I persisted, and after a few weeks and a consultation with my pediatrician, my parents gave me the green light. Like other kids my age, I had seen the comic books with ads showing a guy getting bullied constantly at the beach and then buying this magical product. The guy returns to the beach with muscles and everyone treats him differently.

I was practically drooling with anticipation when we finally went to Venture to buy the weight set. I didn't anticipate the embarrassment that I felt when I couldn't even lift the box into the shopping cart. My mom had to ask the clerk for assistance. I still remember the scornful look the clerk gave me that said: "You kidd'n?"

I had no idea what I was getting into. I had to take the set piece by piece out of my mom's blue Chevy Impala to get it in the house. The set had a cool poster with a breakdown of exercises for beginners, intermediate, and advanced. I proudly hung it on my wall as an immigrant would hang his naturalization documents. Of course, since I had attention deficit issues, I didn't read it other than to notice the movements the artist drew in each box.

I quickly performed the 10-step routine in a matter of minutes, went to eat lunch, and then darted back for another round. By the end of the day, I had completed three rotations of the beginner routine and had cut our grass in between each routine.

 I awoke the next day to my mom's morning ritual of doing dishes in the kitchen, and I immediately understood what the poster meant about only doing one set of each exercise and then waiting a day or two to recover. I could barely walk, sit, or move. Each movement from brushing my teeth to squatting on the toilet exacted a toll. At that point, I decided to read the instructions.

It took me days to recover, but I continued religiously, once I was able to move again. I still had no idea what was happening until three weeks had passed, and my friends started noticing that my 13-year-old physique was changing. They too wanted a slice of this special magical essence. My friends started to come over to work out with me, our group therapy sessions.

THE CARNATION CRUNCHY METAMORPHISIS

Lifting began to take center stage in my life. I altered my eating habits and began reading ingredient labels to find the formula to get bigger quicker. I didn't know the slightest thing about nutrition. To grow, I would devour two McDonald's Quarter Pounders, a large order of fries, and topped it off with an artery-clogging shake.

I consulted my pediatrician, Dr. Seymour Schlansky, whom I held in high regard. He recommended drinking Carnation Instant Breakfast. Since my dad occasionally sold it in his stores, I figured the price was right. I didn't quite understand that sometimes the merchandise in my dad's store was seconds, or "distressed" items, which was the reason why they were a tenth of the price of a regular grocery store.

After drinking packet upon packet of strawberry, vanilla and chocolate malt shakes over that summer, I came to comprehend the meaning of "distressed" goods. Some packets had interesting particles inside. At first I didn't think anything of it and believed that the crunchy flakes in the mix were a part of the composition and flavoring enhancements, part of the "new and improved" as the label read. As the summer months elapsed, I began to recognize the immense similarity they had with cocoons that hung from my dad's fruit trees.

I was always infatuated with butterflies and their metamorphosis from egg to caterpillar to butterfly. And then one day the connection hit me. I opened up a packet after one of my strenuous garage-style workouts and noticed a wiggle or two in one of the crusty things inside. Realization dawned: all those times I had drunk the satisfying shakes, I was getting an extra protein burst from insect supplements.

Over that summer I worked out hard with the plastic weights and even got a bench so the weights wouldn't be so lonely. And lo and behold, when school resumed in the fall, my life was transformed. Those weights did for me what Robert Duvall did for his congregants in the preacher movie, *The Apostle*, they made me a believer. The bullies who had taunted me halted their assaults. The coaches in PE took notice, even coaches Thing One and Thing Two. And yes, girls, girls, girls had a different vision of me. My self-esteem skyrocketed.

MR. FEIBERG, WHERE HAVE YOU BEEN ALL MY LIFE?

There are good teachers, and then there are those that should be sentenced to one of Cambodia's Khmer Rhouge re-education camps. Give a man a toolbox and he thinks he's a carpenter. But just because he has a hammer doesn't necessarily mean he can hit a nail.

By the time our class of troublemakers made it to the ninth grade, some members had ventured into narcotics, others into nicotine, and some lost interest in life. But then our class of misfits received a God-given gift: the real Mr. "Welcome Back Kotter," someone who knew how to teach kids who were disillusioned, or were left out in the rain without a pair of galoshes. In less than an hour, in our very first class, Mr. Feiberg transformed us into doers and producers.

Mr. Feiberg was positive. He didn't yell. He listened to us and complimented us often. Attending his class was a pleasure. For one of the first times in my life, I had someone who didn't mind me being who I was. He could channel our class nuttiness into learning and performing successfully. And yes, for the good of mankind, he sometimes allowed me to deliver a laugh.

Mr. Feiberg's teaching changed my outlook toward school, and for the years remaining, I pretty much passed my courses.

I am thankful today for both good and bad teacher experiences. When we opened our charter school decades later, I could draw upon my encounters with educators. I knew which teachers cared about kids and who was in it for the paycheck; who would go the extra mile, and who would jump off the train the minute the tunnel got dark and the kids started acting up. In this way, I was able to plant good, caring teachers in our school.

I made it out of high school successfully averaging a C. I attended St. Louis Community College at Meramec and earned an associate degree in retailing while continuing to work at Globe Drug. I moved up the food chain to management and built a decent stash of cash in the bank. Still, I had yet to find my footing – my true purpose in life.

While the money was good, I don't think I ever wanted to work retail and wholesale for my entire life. I wanted something more than simply being part of the family business.

And I was still dealing with the damage to my self esteem – from my school experiences and those incidents involving inappropriate touching. I had no one to talk to about any of those issues. Even if you think you can handle the past, it will catch up to you in some way or another.

7

The Man With The Midas Touch

It is people who make this earth a very special and sacred place. Yet first impressions can cloud our minds with prejudice and make us treat people differently. I challenge myself constantly to take people at face value.

On a cloudy, moderately chilly day in January, as I drove out of the garage at Globe Drug, I noticed one of our newer regulars standing outside Globe. He was banging his head against the brick and stone warehouse wall.

At first I smiled and started to laugh. What in the world was he doing? But after watching his stocking covered head bounce back and forth, I couldn't stop thinking, "Damn, that's gotta really hurt."

I slowly passed through the intersection, shaking my head to a similar beat of, "I just don't believe it." I felt a sympathetic headache coming on as I headed home after a long day at work.

I often wondered what I was accomplishing selling candy, liquor, and inexpensive plastic wares. I was earning a nice living, but I didn't feel fulfilled.

Warehouse work during the months of January, February, and March was particularly dismal. To put it mildly, I hated the first quarter; it was always cold. Pockets of frozen air rushed through the warehouse chilling me to the bone.

It happened that on one winter day, after hours of stocking shelves and waiting on customers, I needed to visit the store's bathroom. Now, this was not just any bathroom. Globe Drug's bathroom was an oasis in the inhospitable concrete jungle of downtown St. Louis. Homeless people would stop by, wash up, and warm up, or grab a "power nap" for several hours while occupying a stall. There were six stalls in all, four that were locked because they didn't work, leaving only two available for the employees and the general public. If a couple of homeless people occupied a stall or two on the coldest days, frankly, I just didn't care. I knew that my dad didn't approve, but I also knew that he looked the other way.

On that particular day, I entered the bathroom and heard the warped door handle hit the 80-year-old polished beige marble wall with the usual bang, unaware that my life was about to start a new course. Standing before a urinal, I began to read again the same 10 graffiti words that had been repeatedly painted over and over, only to reappear through the cheap paint that we used. I simultaneously watched the reflection in the long, 12-foot mirror of a man washing his face in one of the many hand bowls.

When I turned to wash my hands, I said hello a couple of times but didn't get a response. I didn't take this personally, because after speaking a third time and still not getting an answer, I realized that it was the same man I had seen hitting his head against the warehouse wall. Perhaps there was something seriously wrong with him.

Several months would pass, and this man would become a regular customer at the store. He banged his head on the wall a couple of times a week, sometimes in the morning, sometimes in the afternoon, whatever worked for his schedule. When I did happen to catch him outside playing a beat on the wall, I started to watch the pedestrians more than him. Some laughed, while others just walked by.

My family had a talent for adapting to our clientele. Every morning, Aunt Rose would separate a one-pound box of saltine crackers into the four factory-wrapped packages and sell them for a quarter a piece. This way a customer could purchase an additional can of 49-cent Vienna sausages and maybe a bottle of Wild Irish Rose. I guess you would say it was the "extra value meal" for the homeless. Yet the guy who beat his head rarely bought the wine; he stuck with the high sodium crackers and the sausages.

As the man became more of a fixture at the store, I would often run into him in the bathroom. But he still wouldn't answer me, wouldn't even look at me. He just stared deep into the mirror, losing himself like a Tibetan monk within the deepest of life's reflections, while occasionally nibbling on a saltine with a wrinkled slice of sausage.

I tried different approaches to opening a dialogue, but to no avail. Humor, rudeness, what have you, still no progress. But one day, I came in to wash my hands and noticed he had left the faucet with the cold water pouring out full blast. I didn't do anything. I left and ate lunch, then returned to the bathroom to brush and floss my teeth only to become a little irritated that the homeless man still had the water on full blast.

I heatedly asked him why he still had the water on and ranted about it being a waste. Finally, after months of silence, he replied, "If you let it run for a while, the water will be colder, because it comes from deeper in the ground." Astonished that he'd finally answered me, my brain fired off numerous disconnected thoughts while I placed a large bead of tricolor-swirled, fluoride toothpaste on my toothbrush.

Since I had no words that were appropriate, I finished brushing and packed my floss and brush back in my crinkled sandwich bag and left. But strangely, a door had been opened.

For some time I had been questioning what I wanted to do in life. Working at the family store seemed more of a convenience than a life goal. I did enjoy much of it: the fast paced action of selling and buying large quantities of everything a factory didn't want; the slice of nine-grain bread, cross-cultural clientele; and the immigrants my Uncle Joe hired by the half-dozen to help with a new start.

I enjoyed talking with the homeless people who frequented the store, and at times I would just throw out thoughts that were troubling me, or some of life's deepest questions. I guess it felt safer to talk about these issues with strangers than with my friends. And maybe I thought I'd get a more realistic answer.

So again, on a day I was feeling pretty down, I happened to pay a visit to the restroom when the head banger was there. Frankly, I don't know what part of my brain this question came from, but it popped out of my mouth as the man's eyes met mine for the first time in months: "Have you seen the light?"

"Which light?" he responded softly.

"Ya know," I said, "the light?"

He jiggled the side pocket on his dusty coat as a light dust flew into the air. He was checking that his vodka was still there, safe and sound, and he repeated, "Which light? There are many lights."

For a second I was startled, because apart from the cold water confrontation, I had received nothing more from him.

"There are different kinds of light. All lights aren't necessarily good. There is bad light out there, too. There is camouflage light, too!" He said all this in one breath, while stroking his nappy beard and looking at himself in the mirror.

Now most people would discount this drunken old bum like a piece of trash, but as for me, I needed to hear some deep words on which to reflect. This time he left the bathroom before I did.

Back at home, I reached into our white kitchen cabinets and grabbed the 750ml of Cuervo Gold. As we touched, it was like holding hands with a loved one, or a field sergeant in battle telling me to hang in there, we are successfully holding the line, despite the casualties.

I poured a generous portion into a glass and shot it back without taking any time to let the aroma penetrate my nostrils. As I reloaded the shot glass that was bought on a ski trip years ago, I asked myself, "Are you drinking just a little too much? Four times in 10 days for someone who rarely gets buzzed?"

My appreciation for alcohol and tendency to self-medicate reentered my life. Years before, I'd had an affair with alcohol and marijuana, but after getting sick and tired of feeling sorry for myself, I had successfully weaned myself off. But here I was again, drinking alone to feel good briefly and escape my depression. I was good at masking it with my wife and friends. It's easy at first, but after a while, people start to notice.

I didn't want to start again, didn't like how I felt, didn't like how the alcohol placed a temporary restraining order on my past, only to have it reemerge more magnified the following day.

The next day, without rhyme or reason or any urge to go to the bathroom, I found myself in there washing my hands, and, of course, the philosopher was leaning on the white sink, sucking on a cheap half-pint of vodka.

I greeted him, and no sooner did I reach for the towels, than he spoke.

"Did ya' do what I said?" he shouted.

"What?" I angrily replied, as if wanting to treat him like the rest of the world.

"Did ya' do what I said?" he repeated.

"'Ya mean look in front of the mirror?" I responded.

"No," he said in a more soothing voice. "I said, did you go back to where it started, where it all began?"

"Yes," I replied, "but I'd have to board a plane to all my sadness."

"Well, change takes time; don't rush things," he said. "You've got to move like the ABCs, in order, don't skip," he continued, while wiping off the top of his bottle. "Do you drink, or do drugs?" he asked quietly, reeling me in deeper.

I realized I had been waiting a long time for someone to ask me that. How did he know to ask? "Ya' know, in fact I have been drinking here and there, but no big thing," I casually explained. "It's not heavy though," I said, looking into his face littered with scars.

"Don't let it catch you," he cautioned softly.

"What do you mean?" I asked.

"Don't let it catch you. It will get you, little at a time, creeps up on ya."

"Watch yourself," he said as I walked out of the bathroom.

A few weeks passed, and my inner conflict heightened with the arrival of spring. Working in a dark, dingy warehouse was a challenge when the outdoors was ready to kick off the concert series of spring flowers, warm sunshine, and virgin leaves.

The next time I ran into the man in the bathroom, I was bolder and just let it out: "Life is hard, so many problems, so much pressure; it's too much!"

His eyes looked at mine through the reflection in the mirror. "You gotta look in the mirror," he said firmly in his deep, rich voice. "Sometimes it's hard to face the mirror to see yourself. It's easy to look at other people and see their problems, but the mirror tells the truth."

So there I was, buckling my pants, and this crazy-looking, gap-toothed, black man seemed to me to be speaking with a lot of truth and insight. I shared my inner thoughts with a stranger, while not trusting friends and family with how sad I was feeling.

"What a mess my life is; what am I doing?"

He paused in thought for a second and replied, "You gotta go back!"

I asked politely, like a good student, "What do you mean?"

"What you need to find out is when these problems started. There was a beginning — go back to when all these problems started. Was it like this all the time? Go back to the point that all this began and see what is causing this." He explained it in a reassuring voice.

I paused as my brain swallowed this refreshing insight. Here were the keys that I needed to unlock my feelings, to figure out how to repair myself and move on.

The man who would bang his head on a six-story warehouse building several times a week, eat 25-cent saltines accompanied by Vienna sausages and wash it down with high octane vodka in a warehouse bathroom, gave me priceless advice for reevaluating my life.

After that encounter, I never saw much of him anymore. I wish that I had at least asked him his name.

8

Dancing With Death

Not long after my talk with that nameless individual, I stood silently in our dark kitchen, waiting, contemplating. I could hear the compressors of our air conditioning units hum in the background as they cooled our house. My feet were as chilled as a perfectly refrigerated salad plate. Waiting, thinking, should I or shouldn't I?

Thoughts raced, memories flashed, jumping at hyper-speed, past ... present, fantasies of departure. My thoughts made doing it seem like a pleasant orgasm, soothing to my fevered mind. It wouldn't hurt.

I knew how I should do it. We all have our styles: mine — a wrist slasher. In my thoughts, my wife emerged, walking into the kitchen to let the dogs out in the early morning, wondering why *I* hadn't let them out ... and then, "Where's Marshall, oh no!" Finding me lying there, on the checkerboard cocoa-brown and faded-white linoleum tiles in a pool of blood. "Will she ever forgive me?" I wondered. "Will she ever understand?"

I wanted out ... completely out. I stood in the entryway to the kitchen, naked, gazing at the decorative knife set in the standard, butcher-block holder. It was a wedding present from my older sister and brother-in-law.

What would my next move be? Would I forfeit the game or move in another direction? I could cry only to myself for help; I was too embarrassed to talk or share what was happening with my understanding and supportive wife.

Should I pray for rescue from my private gulag? What path did I take to get here? Life is so precious, yet three therapists in three years and still no better. Worse, in fact. I'd told the various therapists that I was fine, just to get out of the therapist-patient relationship. Clearly, this wasn't working. It was like seeing a veterinarian for a head cold.

As the chill crept up my feet to my ankles, to my knees, thighs and farther north, I began to shiver a little, as if it were my heart pumping out the last pint. It was a cold feeling that slowly overcame my body. I stared at the blinds. It must be around 2:30 a.m.. I took a fast breath and was ready to get my game on when I suddenly felt my right calf being lightly whipped, as though I were walking through tall weeds.

Looking down, I saw my friend wagging his tail. I could read his mind, "Don't! Please don't! But, while you think about it, do you mind letting me out? I can't hold it anymore!" What a perfect correlation. My Dalmatian needs to relieve his bladder, so he can get back to sleep, while I was anticipating relieving myself in my own way.

As I bent down to give him a big hug, I never wanted to let go. In response to the hug, his tail commenced speed-wagging. The tail thumping against the refrigerator sounded just like my grandmother's old, pivoting metal-blade fan clicking with every revolution. Distracted, I figured I'd go back to bed. Sleep on my next move. I'm too tired, and I haven't had a chance to write apology letters to explain why I was doing what I was doing.

When the dog came back in, I retreated under the covers as though finding sanctuary under a layer of fallen autumn leaves. I was just too tired to think anymore. My spotted friend stood next to the bed looking at me, wagging for one more pat on his coarse black-and-white head. Soon the sun would rise and bring a new set of challenges to my soul.

Six hours later, while at work, and a little rested, I again opened the Yellow Pages and skimmed the list of therapists. As with the previous three, my method of picking someone made no sense and had no logic. Either a name sounded good, or the office wasn't too inconvenient.

I found one with a nice name and an office in Creve Coeur, a St. Louis suburb. I called immediately because I was in a "code-red status" and left a message. He called me back within an hour, and I booked the last appointment of the evening.

It was a few minutes before 8:00 p.m. when I arrived. Like his predecessors, this one shared the office with several other therapists. I stared at the usual decorations found in a waiting room, calming things like a vase with plastic flowers, an assortment of articles, and framed pictures to dress out the space. A few chairs were sprinkled in a crooked semi-circle and the typical pamphlets on everything from adolescent behavior, alcoholism, and 'what is causing unusual mood swings.'

He opened the door, and we made brief introductions while shaking hands. I thanked him for seeing me at the last minute. Little did he know how thankful I was; or, maybe he did. After all, that's the nature of his business. He asked if I was putting this on my insurance. I said, no, I would pay as we go. I didn't want it "out there" that I was seeing anyone.

He led me to his private office and asked how he could help as we simultaneously sat down. My butt had only wiggled a millisecond in the chair before I told him without hesitation that I was going to commit suicide.

He leaned forward to listen and probably didn't have an inkling his last appointment of the night was going to be an intense one. I'm quite sure I stirred his energy level up a notch or two. I went into my sales mode of asking for a two-hour session instead the standard one-hour. He agreed. I'm sure for the price that I was paying he didn't have a problem with it.

We clicked immediately, and the two-hour session passed quickly. I felt relieved and walked out of the appointment smiling knowing that committing suicide, as appealing and appetizing as it was to me before the session, would have been the most rotten thing I could have done to myself and to all the people in my life. I just needed someone who could talk my talk. Over the course of a couple of months, he got me to a safe place and a different frame of mind.

9

Marketing 101

I stood perched at my counter in the store. Our eyes briefly collided. He was searching for discount laundry soap, while I was looking for a kid to ask about my far-fetched idea. I felt sure I couldn't go wrong. What kid wouldn't like the idea?

As I approached, he was bent slightly forward, scanning the bottles of bleach and getting ready to make a decision: Clorox or the discount 69-cent brand?

"Can I help you?" I asked in my stock salesman voice.

"I'm get'n some soap powder," he responded.

"Do you live around here?"

"Yeah, my brothers and me and my mama stay in the projects."

Our conversation continued to dance for a while until I finally popped the question. "I'm opening a gym for kids...you know, like your age...to lift weights and body build, like Arnold Schwarzenegger. You think you'd be interested?"

His eyes lit up. "When are you goin' to open it? Man, I always wanted muscles!"

"Come back in a couple of weeks, and I'll let you know when....Oh, you think you can pay $2.50 a week for the membership fee?" I asked as an afterthought.

"Oh yeah, that's nothin'." He waved his hand to reassure me that it was a piddly amount.

"What's your name?"

"Raymond!" he exclaimed as he turned to the checkout with the discount "soap powder," as he called it. "See you," he called back as he walked away.

At college, I barely scraped together a C in Marketing. All I knew now was that I couldn't take working at my family's store much longer. The 60-

plus hours a week were taking a toll on me. Even more, I couldn't take the constant news reports from Peter Jennings about the surge in street gangs and how crack cocaine use was overtaking large swaths of low-income neighborhoods.

I chose power lifting and weightlifting because although lifting isn't a glamorous sport, a person can excel simply by training hard. You didn't have to rely on another team member, as in basketball, to carry the weight. Kids could take charge of their own destiny. And all you need are a minimal number of weights to train. What better formula could there be: poor kids with nothing to do plus a gym full of weights equals positive self-esteem. So, no, I didn't do any R&D or marketing in advance. All I knew was that I had to do this. It also seemed like it would be a lot of fun.

After the brief exchange with Raymond, I withdrew to my desk to figure out a game plan, starting with where to have the gym, what equipment to buy, and where to buy it. Two hours and many phone calls later, I lifted my head, and there stood Raymond 20 feet away back in the "soap powder" aisle again, but this time with a couple of sidekicks.

"Hey! 'Scuse me!" he politely called over. "My friends want to know when is you goin' to open that gym you was tell'n me about? 'Ya think next week?"

"Maybe in a few," I replied.

"Oh…, well uh…, we'd be interested in com'n'!"

After they left, I knew I needed to follow through with my plan. If he was interested enough to walk on one of the city's longest viaducts back to the housing projects to gather a couple of friends and head all the way back to the store, something must be going on, some type of motivation. Perhaps a gym might be a good idea.

Wheeling and dealing at Globe Drug.

A ROOM WITH A VIEW

When I'm in doubt about life and need a resource, I head to the local flea market to find the answer. There was an auctioneer who was a regular fixture at Globe. "Memphis," as he was called in the world of flea markets and swap meets, was probably the only black auctioneer in this region back in the day. Yet he fit in well because he wore a mangled cowboy hat that blended in with the other rural auctioneers. When his hat was knocked off while loading his late '70s Dodge van, his overgrown Afro was molded into the shape of the interior of the hat.

Next to my Aunt Rose, Memphis was the best salesperson ever. People bought what he was hustling, regardless of the condition, purely because of his entertaining sales pitch.

He also knew a lot of people, legitimate and illegitimate, and I had the feeling he could lead me to a place to house the gym. He was your "go-to guy" for anything halfway legal. He guided me to a place on Washington Avenue in downtown St. Louis, just a little off the beaten path, not too far from Globe. He said he knew the owner and thought he could swing a deal.

That afternoon, I drove by the location. It was a long building that looked like a Swiss chalet in the Alps, only without the snow, without the altitude, and without the tourists. It had multiple storefronts, and I noticed some hand-made signs. I went back to my apartment to contact the owner. Because of the array of boarded up windows, I assumed that the price would be right.

The man answering the phone seemed genuinely interested in renting the space. My concern was that he might not want to rent it to someone who would be hosting a bunch of city kids. They might scare off the customers of other tenants. Little did I know that he needed the revenue stream just as badly as I needed the space. He said he could give me a large space for around $250 a month. I liked the price and couldn't imagine not making enough money to cover the rent and expenses.

We met the next afternoon at the building. He led me to a 3,000-square-foot area that he believed "would be a good space for the gym." He opened a door flanked by a couple of windows boarded up with bowed plywood.

Like a gunslinger, he pulled out a flashlight and we proceeded inside. Above us was a gorgeous, original tin ceiling degraded by a couple of temporary light fixtures that wiggled in the wind as we opened the door. A few mice scurried for cover. I knew the location would work, and, for the life of me, just couldn't figure out why he was so desperate to rent it out, and why the price was so below market.

We agreed to meet the next day to sign the lease. Normally, a sensible person wouldn't hand over money before getting a business license and obtaining the correct permits. But I was going to open this place regardless of what permits were needed.

I ordered the weight equipment and proudly wrote a check for $9,200 and mailed it to the factory. To this day I wonder what the hell could possibly have been going through my mind. Wouldn't a nice new car be a better option?

Prior to the equipment arriving, I hired Tommy, Danny, Mike, and Bob, the homeless brigade I knew from the store. On any given day, this group was inebriated more than they were sober. I turned them loose with sledgehammers to tear out a few walls and clean up and fix several other things. Since they were drunk, they occasionally missed the walls and damaged some fixtures. At first I was upset, but it actually worked better than I had envisioned. I almost passed out from the stench coming off their soiled clothes. But this crew fit my budget, while they, in turn, got a kick out of helping to get the place set up.

At the time, Tommy was fresh out of prison, and the muscles he had developed during his incarceration hadn't yet eroded, so he was a pretty strong worker. He was also encouraging about the idea of kids working out and building their self-esteem.

After the demolition was done, it took a couple of weeks to plaster and paint, install an inexpensive green Astroturf floor, and hang mirrors and cool posters of steroid enhanced athletes that you get in those bodybuilding magazines. We attempted to paint the ceiling, but every time we rolled the paint on, older paint underneath caused the fresh paint to fall to the concrete floor below. We gave up on that. Our space began to look a lot like Rocky Balboa's primitive gym in downtown Philadelphia.

Finally the equipment arrived, and my childhood days watching Laurel and Hardy movies returned to me. You'll recall the piano delivery scene up long, steep stairs? I had a group of Stan Laurels and Oliver Hardys helping out that day. The weight machines were unloaded between shots of cheap domestic vodka and swigs of Mogen David. When we tried to lift in unison with the standard, "okay, on three," we could never get our rhythm right. One would pull while the other pushed; one raised as the other lowered.

And then, the occasional movement of internal gas that accompanied the move cracked us all up. It was truly a symphony of kinesthetics. No doubt, someone walked away from the experience with a popped hernia. Eventually, after many hours that should have taken a few, we unloaded and assembled all the equipment. The aesthetics might not have been up to par, but what our gym lacked in polish, it made up for in energy.

On the day that we opened, Raymond brought several of his friends. I told them that the first week would be free; after that, it would cost them $2.50 a week. They agreed, and I took them through a workout. They enjoyed seeing their pumped up muscles in the mirrors. They were eager to go through the workout again and really wanted to do more; but, remembering my own first experience years before, I warned them repeatedly to wait until the next day, because they would be sore.

The very next day, Raymond came to see me at the store after school. "Man, I'm so sore, I even had trouble going to the bathroom." He smiled broadly while touching his arms. After just the first workout, you could tell he was hooked.

We were off to a great start - except, like in many parts of the country, St. Louis has this thing called rain. I came to realize why the space was only $250 a month. As the storms arrived, water began to pour in at least a dozen places. This wasn't your typical drip here, and drip there — the place was flooded.

The landlord acted surprised at my pacnicked calls. I also called Memphis and yelled at him for no justifiable reason. He suggested I slide the equipment away from the leaks and put some buckets out. "Brilliant," I thought to myself, "if only I had a dozen buckets."

A month passed, and every time it rained the place looked like an indoor water park. By now it was clear the owner wasn't going to fix it, or anything else that popped up.

KEEP YOUR FRIENDS CLOSE AND YOUR ENEMIES CLOSER

Word of the new gym spread quickly. My friends, acquaintances and neighbors were more than a little dubious.

I remember one Globe customer in particular, a regular who owned a corner store in a dangerous part of town. As an African-American, he had plenty of opinions about what was wrong with the black community; "Too many storefront churches and liquor stores. There's one on every dang corner."

When I told him that I had opened a gym for kids, he lowered his head so he could peer at me above his glasses and said, "You did what?"

I explained the idea and how for $2.50 a week kids could get off the streets and stay out of trouble.

"Well, when you save the city and close up after a month, let me know. I'll buy all the equipment for a good price."

Some of my white friends made negative comments, too. They thought the only thing the gym would do is make these black kids stronger so they could rob us. One person told me that there were Jewish kids without fathers, and I should go help them instead.

The barrage of negative remarks saddened me. I was disappointed that people I thought were my friends, who "had my back," were in fact talking behind my back. I was hurt they had so little faith in my plans. Under no circumstances would I let the naysayers prevail.

With the start of the second week, Raymond was back and eager to workout. While he was bench pressing, it hit me that I had forgotten to ask him for his membership dues. I approached him as he was pushing the weight off his chest.

"Umm," he paused, "can I pay you next time? I left my money at home."

I didn't think much of it and said okay. But when he returned later that week, I asked him why his friends hadn't returned. He shrugged it off and said they were busy. I again asked for his membership fee. He promised to bring it "tomorrow."

The next day, Raymond showed up, still without his friends. At that point I knew something was wrong. Before we started to workout, I again asked him for his $2.50.

"I'll be your cleanup guy!" he proposed eagerly. "I'm a good cleaner. I clean at my Momma's all the time."

So there I stood, scratching my head in a two-bit, $250-a-month warehouse space with more than nine grand of my own money sunk into weight equipment, surrounded by barbells, dumbbells, boarded up windows, and plastic buckets strategically placed for the onslaught of the next rainstorm. Heck, I didn't even have the correct permit to be officially open. I thought to myself, "Will the real dumbbell please step forward?"

And there was Raymond, looking down at the floor in embarrassment. "Um, can I be your cleanup guy?"

I hired Raymond and dropped the $2.50 membership fee. His buddies returned the following week.

10

Kol Nidre

Sooner or later, most people are confronted with life's most compelling question: Is there a God? I try to keep a strong belief. Sometimes, though, I feel God is out to get me and teach me a damn good lesson.

That lesson arrived in the form of Eugene, a disheveled, Hassidic-looking man who may have been the only Jewish homeless person in the St. Louis area. After I met Eugene, we had spectacular conversations about business, politics, and a variety of other subjects. He was brilliant. After I learned that he was homeless, I decided I needed to "lend a hand." I was

Big weekend for Raymond: first time on an airplane and 3rd place at a bodybuilding contest in Springfield, Missouri, 1991.

determined to find him a better place to sleep than the local transit system.

Eugene's sleep pattern was interesting — he set a standard as a power napper. Instead of sleeping eight hours at a time, he dozed off on the bus and woke up whenever it stopped. When the bus continued, he would fall asleep again. You have to remember that some stops might have been two blocks apart. If he was really exhausted and overslept, he would miss his destination and have to ride the route a second time.

My parents tried to help Eugene. Dad would give him his leftover lunches. When the relationship grew stronger, my mom, bless her heart, started packing Eugene his own lunches with raisin kugel, twice-baked potatoes, assortments of soft fruits past their prime, and low-salt matzo ball soup. Had you witnessed Eugene eating you'd realize what a true blessing food is, worth more than all the gold in the world.

I went to extremes to get Eugene assistance from the government and get him off the streets. I would get in trouble with my uncles and aunts when Eugene hung out at the store all day, napping or getting on everyone's nerves. Finding him a low cost apartment would help him stay safe at night. Although it was a thankless task, I found that I enjoyed maneuvering around Big Brother's system.

One thing I knew: Eugene needed to get off the streets and receive assistance fast. The first requirement for obtaining disability was a medical exam, but getting in to see a doctor was going to take months. We didn't have time for that, so I called an osteopath, thinking he might not be as heavily booked. I found one in a financially challenged neighborhood and took Eugene in for a physical. The examining room was quite intimate, more suited to a family-owned Italian restaurant than a medical facility.

The examination went off without a hitch. The doctor checked his height and weight, listened to his heart, took his blood pressure and scanned his body for disorders—whatever was required to take Eugene to the next level. The physician was nice, if he was one. To this day, I'm not certain of his qualifications. Regardless, he asked the one important question, "Why are you getting an examination?" I replied that Eugene was trying to get disability. With that, and half a glance at Eugene, it was a done deal.

The next step was to find a psychiatrist to evaluate Eugene. I found one who had a cancellation, and Eugene and I dropped everything to make the appointment. While sitting in the waiting room, I bet myself that the evaluation wouldn't last more than three questions before the doctor signed off on the papers certifying Eugene disabled. Once Eugene started talking, it would seal his entry in the system of disabled Americans. Luckily, Eugene was in one of his intensified mood swings of manic enlightenment.

No sooner had the doctor asked for his name and address, than Eugene countered with a series of questions of his own, pumping the doctor for information about what psychiatric conferences he'd recently attended. You see, Eugene's own specialty was going to conventions, fairs, and other events listed in business and medical journals. From frozen food trade shows to art gallery ribbon cuttings, you could count on Eugene to be in attendance.

Eugene could obtain an ID when conventioneers tossed their badges in the trash on the way out. He would then stroll the convention floor in his casual convention outfit of wrinkled Docker khakis and the $1.99-three-sizes-too-big bowling shoes from Globe.

Food shows naturally held a particular allure. At one, Eugene walked around for a week wearing a badge from Kraft Foods with the name of Cynthia H. hanging off his crumpled, cotton-knit shirt. I've tried to imagine what the pitchmen at the various booths thought when approached by this senior with the name of Cynthia H., of Kraft Foods, International Division.

Eugene simply loved to gather information, all kinds of information. With the Washington University School of Medicine nearby, he had attended lectures by some of the nation's most notable psychiatrists and therapists. He looked like Einstein's half-brother. Who would challenge him?

The doctor interrupted Eugene to ask the stock psychiatric evaluation questions, like whether he could count backwards from 100 by odd numbers, or name three presidents. Eugene responded, "From which country?" and that solidified the deal for the doctor as he scribbled some notes on the evaluation sheet. I don't doubt that Eugene could have named three presidents from probably a dozen countries. In any event, the psychiatrist made his determination, and Eugene eventually started receiving his disability checks.

Eugene was constantly talking to eager salesmen that he either met at a convention or from one of the many calls that he made to the new 800 numbers that were the rage prior to the internet. Some didn't bother to investigate his claims. One time Eugene contacted a casket company and told a representative that we had an empty warehouse floor that we were interested in filling up with caskets for wholesaling out to the public. I wish I could have heard that conversation.

Public bankruptcy hearings were also on Eugene's social calendar. He was particularly troubled that the failure of the *Globe Democrat* would leave St. Louis with just one daily paper. Naturally he felt it his civic duty to attend that hearing.

As a formality in the bankruptcy hearing, the judge asked the packed courtroom, "Is there anyone here able to buy out the *Globe Democrat*, or does anyone have claims against the *Globe*?" The courtroom was quiet until Eugene stood and proudly, like he was Patton giving a speech before the battle of the Bulge, stated, "The Cohen boys at Globe Drug wish to buy the paper!" as he slammed his fist in his hand.

Now I'm sure that most everyone found Eugene's statement surprising, but not nearly as surprising as the attorneys representing the shuttered *Globe Democrat*, who coincidentally happened to be my uncles' and dad's attorneys, too.

I never heard the end of that from my Uncle Joe. But Eugene's offsetting charm and tsunami mood swings made him one of the most interesting people I have ever known.

As problematic as Eugene was, he was a righteous man. I cherished the conversations we had. He taught me things that you can't read in a book, like the persistence and maneuverability required to become successful. He always believed it was possible to implement any idea and he steadfastly supported any idea that I shared with him, regardless of how outlandish it was. When some family and friends poked fun at my idea of opening a gym for kids, Eugene was behind it 100 percent. Eugene believed so much that anything in life was possible, he once entered the 17th ward aldermanic race or as he called it, 'neighborhood mayor' and garnered over 100 votes without any formal campaign. Of course, I gave him my vote.

Eugene hung out regularly at the gym after it opened, which was good because the kids had never been in contact with an elderly Jewish man, let alone one with a yarmulke that regularly fell off his head. Eugene would pedal our donated, crooked exercise bike backward and lift a five-pound dumbbell in ways that would make an exercise physiologist cringe. But in Eugene's mind, he was exercising and we all enjoyed the company.

After two years of operating the gym, I was more committed than ever to providing a safe place for inner city kids to work out, play, and just hang out and escape for a while from the static around them.

I opened the gym as many days as I could, even on holidays if the kids expressed an interest. They called me regularly during the day to check whether the gym would be open. You could sense from their voices the need, the desire they had to come to this shoddy oasis. The kids would even come to Globe Drug when school let out and wait until I would drive them to the gym in my dented, dull black, 12-year-old Camaro with a single white replacement door from a previous accident.

But one evening, as I started loading up the car with a small platoon of kids, a booming voice echoed through the dimly lit warehouse parking garage. *"Where do you think you are going?"*

It was Eugene.

"We're headed to the gym."

"To the gym!" he roared back with the rage of a prophet.

"Yeah, I'm only going to open it up for a little bit," I said defensively.

"It's Kol Nidre — Yom Kippur — the holiest day of the year, the Day of Atonement!" He leaned his head forward, looking above the brim of his glasses to make eye contact with me, like my third grade teacher would do right before pulling my left ear for bad behavior. I hesitated and then quickly shrugged him off.

Eugene turned to the doorway, both hands holding a double-layered shopping bag stuffed with periodicals. "God will punish you for this."

Eugene faded down the cobblestone alley and went to his bus stop to head to Hillel at Washington University for the free worship service. The kids asked, "What's Gene's deal?" I shrugged it off as nothing too important.

"Let's get out of here and get our game on." We rumbled down the alley, passing Eugene as we rounded the corner, and half-heartedly waved goodbye.

My stomach rumbled from hunger. A half-hour had passed at the gym, and I thought we could stay perhaps another hour or so before I could dart home to devour an assortment of food before sundown that would last me through the Yom Kippur fast. No sooner had I considered the position of the sun in the sky relative to nightfall than Raymond appeared, brandishing in my face a ripped, imitation Everlast, red boxing glove. Raymond's exposed knuckle was bleeding.

Raymond's sparring partner, Lonnie, meanwhile, was bent over the Astro Turf floor covered with blood, pouring from a lip that was hinged half off his face. As Lonnie cried hysterically, I told one of the kids to run to the Chinese restaurant across the street and request enough ice for both injuries. We placed the "field dressing" ice packets on Lonnie's face and listened to him screech.

I ushered everyone into my Camaro and sped off to Cardinal Glennon

Children's Hospital. The emergency room was as jammed as a country carnival.

The clerk motioned us to sit. I was flanked by Raymond and Lonnie, each with blood-soaked clothes, and accompanied by Lonnie's pained whimpering. No matter, the lady typing had seen it all. She asked if I was the parent or guardian, and I naturally replied that I wasn't.

"Well we can't admit anyone without a parent or guardian."

Disjointed thoughts surged through my mind: *Shit, my car is 5,000 miles overdue for an oil change! I think my fast is going to start early, because I won't get a chance to eat, so can I end my fast earlier than sundown? Most of these kids don't have working telephones — how in the world will I get in touch with their parents?*

So I got on the phone and began to reach out to the kids' extended families. I called Lonnie's cousin's grandmother's house and left a message that I would call back in ten minutes after they'd had a chance to go across the street and up the stairs in the next housing project to relay the message to Lonnie's mother. After a volley of phone calls, I finally made contact with his mother. She said she had time to come but didn't have a car or a ride. I told her I would be there in 10 minutes.

Raymond's mother did have a working telephone. Ms. Moore said she would come to the hospital shortly. I then hopped in my car and darted downtown to the projects to pick up Lonnie's mother. I pulled into the parking lot of the cluster of high-rises and waited for her to come out of one of them. I left my car running and honked the horn a couple of times, hoping that she was an on-time person.

As I waited, I noticed a thin, desolate looking man dressed in logo sportswear appear at the entrance to the fenced parking lot. At first I thought he was just walking by, but when he made eye contact with me, I realized he was either going to beg me for a buck or two to buy some malt liquor or attempt to sell me a small batch of narcotics, something I wasn't remotely interested in.

I waved him off like a persistent mosquito and noticed Lonnie's mother walking out of a building and heading toward my car. As the peddler finally got the message that my window wasn't opening, he walked off down the street. I was reminded of my mother's constant lectures about keeping your car windows and doors locked at all times. With that thought in mind, I leaned and opened the passenger side door for Lonnie's mother.

No sooner had her starched jeans hit the passenger seat than an odd collection of undercover cars, housing security vehicles, and a police car or two surrounded us. I blinked a couple of times to make sure I wasn't in a Clint Eastwood "Dirty Harry" movie.

"Put your hands out of the car and don't move!" The boot camp voice was coming from somewhere behind the vehicles. I tried to locate its source in my rear view mirror and happened to glance at Lonnie's mother's face. I recognized a familiar look of hopelessness and anger.

"Step out of the car!" the voice barked again. Lonnie's mom and I cooperated, emerging from the car like a synchronized swimming duo.

"Step behind the car!" the plainclothes person said, as I tried to figure out if he was a police officer, a postal inspector, or a wannabe FBI agent.

"How long have you been coming here to buy?" he demanded.

"What are you talking about?" I responded in a frantically nerdy voice. "This is unbelievable!"

The undercover officer then inserted half of his upper torso inside my driver's window like a magician performing a delicate magic trick and re-appeared with his thumb and index finger proudly displaying a tiny white crystal. "What's this?" he triumphantly intoned, as if he had just cracked the biggest case of his early crime-fighting life.

I walked up to get a closer glimpse, squinted a couple of times, and asked in an ignorant, suburban Jewish voice that didn't know squat about ghetto life, "What's that? How did that get in there?"

"Oh c'mon," nudged the officer.

"What the hell is that? You gotta be kidding me?"

The scene drew the attention of several basketball players on the makeshift asphalt court that flanked where we were parked.

"Hey, Marshall's getting busted!"

"Marshall got caught!"

I guess you could say they were supporters of mine; some were kids from the gym.

"This is crazy!" I ranted. "You gotta be kidding me! I'm picking her up to take her to Cardinal Glennon Children's Hospital, because her son is injured. Call the hospital!"

The undercover officer didn't respond, so I continued, "I didn't come here to buy anything. My dad knows all the officers that work downtown." This time I pointed to Globe Drug, which was in view just over the viaduct. "Call the hospital," I repeated, "they'll tell you."

The cadre of officers and security guards huddled around one of the unmarked cars for over ten minutes before the officer came back. "You can go; let's just keep this between ourselves."

I didn't answer, but we both got back in my car shaking our heads in disbelief, and drove off to the hospital.

We finally reached the emergency room, where Ms. Moore had been waiting with Raymond, who already wore a plastic wrist band ID. Lonnie's mother went through the paperwork routine. It wasn't long before they called both patients to separate rooms. I decided to go with Lonnie, because his injury was more severe.

Now I was kind of new to this. Although I'd been to Disneyland, Knott's Berry Farm, Six Flags, you name it, I still hadn't learned that just 'cause you round the bend and get closer to the ride, doesn't mean you're on the ride. A nurse called us into a room, where they asked some stock questions, checked weight, blood pressure, the typical stuff, and then we got to wait some more.

Maybe 40 minutes passed, and we were called into another room, where a doctor finally examined the wound, asked more questions, smiled and said he'd be back. And we waited again.

Another 30 or 40 minutes passed while it become clearer to me that not only had I missed the opportunity to eat before the fast, it was doubtful I would make the Kol Nidre service at all. As soon as the doctor entered the room, I got an idea that we would be getting down to business, yet he'd only returned to say that, because it was a facial injury, an expert was needed to sew Lonnie's hinged lip back on his face.

While waiting for the plastic surgeon, I walked down the hall to check on Raymond, who had his hand soaking in a blue fluorescent liquid. Raymond bragged, "I'm going to need to get it stitched up." I said, "Oh," and reassured him that I was down the hall.

About 10 minutes later, the surgeon came in and introduced himself. His name was familiar to me. Dr. David German. When he pulled the gauze away from Lonnie's face, the boy yelped like an injured dog. Dr. German proclaimed that he was going to stitch Lonnie up. As he turned to leave the room to get his equipment, I asked if he was the same person who lived down the street from us as kids. He affirmed that he was. We played the geography game for several seconds, and he left the room.

When he returned with his small stitch kit, accompanied by a medley of long and short syringes, he told Lonnie that he was going to give him a series of shots to his lip and that it was going to hurt. Lonnie asked how many shots, and the doctor said at least six. With that you would have thought you were in an Italian opera house. Lonnie's wails could be heard down the corridor, down the elevator shaft, clear across to the gas station on the other side of the street, and the doctor hadn't even given him his first shot yet.

The doctor eased Lonnie down on the exam table. He told Lonnie's mother to hold his head down, while I was instructed to pinion his arms. He then began to administer shots of painkiller to the 13-year-old's lip. The screams pierced my heart, but not as strongly as his angry mother's look pierced my gut. Her face said, "First I'm going to kill you, and then I'm going to sue you."

Lonnie scored 44 stitches to Raymond's twelve. When we left the hospital, I drove Lonnie and his mother home, this time without police interference.

Lonnie's mother did not sue and, oddly enough, Lonnie's lower lip looked better than the one he was born with. I learned a great deal from that night, or should I say nightmare. I should have listened to Eugene. From that point on, I have closed the gym for Yom Kippur, the Day of Atonement.

In 2009, Eugene Starr moved into a nursing home and lived there until passing away on February 1, 2013.

Eugene and a friend enjoy a Christmas party at the gym.

II

Marathon Man

"Great set!" I said to Raymond as he placed the dumbbells on the mat. He smiled back, flexed his pecs as he leaned into the mirror, and told Tom it was his turn. Tom Metcalf sat curled over on the next bench, clutching his cheek as if he'd just been smacked.

"Tom, it's your turn; what's wrong man?" Raymond said.

"My mouth is hurting," Tom groaned while grabbing the weights.

"I think I have a cavity, or something," he said as he lay back down and began swinging the dumbbells off the bench hoping the short-term pump in his muscles would replace the pain from his jaw.

I didn't pry much further until I took Tom home. In the car I asked why his mother didn't take him to the dentist. He said she was trying to make an appointment, but he didn't know when it would be.

"When was the last time you went to a dentist?"

"It's been some years."

"Like a year or two?"

"No, I think it was about when I was around six."

"So you haven't been to the dentist in six years or so?" I asked with a hint of anger as my car stopped in front of his run down apartment.

"Yeah, I guess." He opened the door to leave.

"I think you can go to the clinic for free if you call for an appointment. Why don't you ask your Mom?"

"I'll ask her again. See you later." He swung the door closed and threw his lopsided book bag over his shoulder as he headed to his apartment.

As I drove off, I shook my head. Whatever happened to visiting the dentist twice a year for checkups? But then I remembered that I had lived a cookie cutter – Beaver Cleaver life.

A week passed, and during another workout, Tom was wiggling his jaw again.

"Did your mom call the dentist, yet?"

"She said she was goin' to," he replied as he grabbed the dumbbells for another set of curls.

Here we go again, I thought to myself. It will never get done.

"How can you sleep at night with that pain?" I persisted.

"Sometimes I wake up a lot. But it's hard to concentrate at school."

At that point I tapped into my inner social worker. "I think I know of a place that I can take you. Do you think if I set up an appointment, your mom will let me take you?"

"Yeah, probably," he replied.

The next day I got on the phone and called a local university with a dental program. I had heard they provided a free clinic for the community. Their green dental students would work with patients under the direction of teaching dentists.

After being transferred around the campus like a carousel, I finally reached the office that made dental appointments. I asked about the procedure and was told to have the parent or guardian present at the appointment to fill out the necessary paperwork. We agreed on a date, and I called Tom's mom. She said that she could bring him but asked if she could follow me in my car to the appointment. I replied that it wouldn't be a problem and gave her the date, which was two weeks away.

Tom was one of the very first gym members. He enjoyed the attention he received from his teachers, kids on the block, and everyone else who noticed how big and strong he was getting. At 13, he was a super athlete with a super attitude. And a good role model. Tom enjoyed coming to the gym after school, while so many of his counterparts were hustling crack cocaine on the street.

What made Tom different? I can only say that he was a good kid with a good mother. His mom had a solid job and provided stability. The only thing Tom lacked was a safe place to go after school. We provided that at the gym. He won many awards in the lifting and track meets we entered.

Tom's work ethic and athletic ability should have been enough to land him on any select team. But his choices were limited by poverty. Nevertheless, I knew Tom could make it.

Tom was always the first to the gym and the last to leave. He helped clean up and assisted with anything else I asked. He loved lifting and couldn't comprehend when I closed the gym on holidays like Memorial Day and the Fourth of July. Exercising was essential in his life of limited opportunity.

Two weeks passed and I called Tom's mom to remind her about the next day's dental appointment. When I pulled up to their apartment at the designated time, sure enough, Tom and his mother were there waiting for me to lead the caravan to his first dental appointment in over six years.

Tom's mother filled out the necessary paperwork while we waited. Time passed rather quickly from the time Tom went into the examining room until his return. They gave him the standard x-ray and cleaning. A student dentist came over to tell me that Tom needed to come in for another appointment, so they could fill four cavities.

I knew that it would be difficult for Tom's mother to take off work again. She was paid hourly and couldn't afford to lose even a half-hour more time. So I asked her if she would mind my taking him to the next appointment. Since Tom was spending regular time at the gym, his mother knew she could trust me. She thanked me for the offer and proceeded to give the nurse permission for me to bring him.

The next appointment came quickly. I picked Tom up mid-morning, and before he even sat down in the car, he thanked me for taking him to get his teeth "fixed."

I replied that it was no problem and that once he had the cavities taken care of, he wouldn't be in any more pain. He told me his mother had been giving him Anbesol and it helped take a little of the pain away.

We arrived at the appointment on time, checked in with the nurse, and sat down among the dozen or so others waiting for free treatment.

The door to the examining room opened repeatedly, and a collection of young dental students in starched-white lab coats called the next patient, slowly picking off people in the waiting room one by one.

As each dental student announced a name and disappeared down the long hallway, I noticed that each seemed to be from a different part of the world because of their mild to thick accents.

When they finally whittled the list down to Tom, a tiny, small-framed woman with chart in hand called out his name in a thick accent. Tom and I stood up in unison and approached the dental student as she generously smiled at Tom to make him feel comfortable, having probably learned it in the first week of Dental 101. I asked Tom if he needed me to go in with him, but Tom assured me, "That's okay, you can wait out here."

I sat down to wait and reread the fancy propaganda about good dental hygiene that was strewn around the assorted tables. Since it was lunch time, my stomach began a symphony of bubbles and growls.

Tom and the dental student returned about an hour later. Tom was rubbing his jawbone as though petting a guinea pig that was trying to wiggle and squirm away. I asked how it went, but before I got an answer I couldn't help noticing the dental student looked rather distressed.

She paused for a moment before answering: "I asked him if he wanted something for the pain, but he didn't want any."

"So you filled all four cavities?"

"Yes, but I've never seen any of the patients not want pain medicine. I kept asking, but he didn't want any," she said with her voice rising.

"He didn't want Novocaine or something like that?"

"No," she said in disbelief. "He didn't even move that much when we were drilling."

I looked at Tom, who sat down next to me with his head down. He looked like a kid who had been eagerly anticipating a visit to a farm to see cuddly barnyard animals only to be shocked by a bunch of chickens running around with their heads chopped off.

Putting it politely, I figured there was a slight language gap between Tom's local street hood lingo and her Indian accent.

But the damage was done. You would think the somewhat timid dental student would have insisted on giving something to a 13-year-old boy with no knowledge of pain control regimen. Perhaps I should have pressed to go into the room with him.

Do you remember the movie, *Marathon Man*, when Lawrence Olivier administers some unconventional dental treatment to Dustin Hoffman? I never intended for poor Tom to reprise Hoffman's role.

With Tom's teeth now painfully repaired, we drove off to grab a small collection of tacos and burritos at the Del Taco next door. Tom thanked me again for taking him to the dentist and for refilling our empty stomachs.

"I'm glad these cavities are finally filled. I'm going to make sure I get to the dentist to clean my teeth a couple of times a year," he said. "But I couldn't understand what that lady was saying to me," he said shaking his head, while fooling with the radio volume. "She just didn't make sense."

Tom (left), Raymond and I at The Show-Me State Games, 1989.

12

Twizzlers

After shelving yet another case in an endless series of canned goods, I glanced up and noticed a kid, around 11 or 12, make his way into the restroom at Globe Drug. Since the restroom provided a refuge for goniffs trying to help themselves to free merchandise, I quickly put down my box cutter and followed him in. I entered just in time to catch him sliding a 12-ounce pack of Strawberry Twizzlers down his baggy pants.

"You know, you don't have to steal it. Don't do that kind of stuff!"

"I'm sorry," he replied convincingly while pulling the half-sunk bag out of his pants. His baby face was very appealing and seemed to say, "Hey, I'm really a nice kid."

As the moment of uncomfortable silence evaporated, I asked, "Why don't you come to the gym down on Washington and 20th street? Raymond comes all the time. You know Raymond?"

"Yeah, I know him."

"I always make a pickup at the projects around 4:45 p.m. in a black Camaro. It's got a white door."

"Okay, I'll be there," he said.

With that I flung the sack of Twizzlers back to him, barely missing the urinal. As he caught it he said, "Thanks, why'd ya do that?"

"Just promise not to steal in this store anymore."

"Okay, I won't," he responded with a sparkle in his eye.

The bridge was built: white Jew, black kid, trust.

Our relationship grew over the months that A came to the gym and enjoyed the "pump" he got from the workouts. I visited his school to check up on his grades. I garnered an extreme honor when he received free tickets to basketball games for good grades and attendance and he selected me to go with him.

Though A and I were making progress in the gym and at school, his family life was a disaster in the making. With an alcoholic mom who was incoherent 90% of the time, A was like a stray dog running loose. The streets raised him. If you cannot respect your mom, how can you respect anything in life? As he grew older, he often confronted his mother, telling her things like, "You don't run me, bitch."

A soon learned that driving was appealing and enjoyable. The only problem was that 13 is a bit too early to start. He began to "borrow" cars for short power drives until the gas tank went empty. Joyriding consumed his time instead of going to school.

A had another mentor besides me, a man named Al, who spent considerable time with him. Al took him on outings and helped him find small jobs like cutting grass in the hope the money would help A stay straight. Al and I spoke regularly. We were both frustrated with the damage A was doing to himself and the community.

We knew A had an older brother stationed in New Jersey, a career Army guy. The brother was married, had an 8-year-old, and was living a good life. He was attending college in preparation for his post-military life.

I called his brother when I found out A had broken into an apartment in the projects. Maybe it was time for A to have a change of scenery. After two weeks of negotiations, A's brother agreed to open his home to his younger sibling. I felt like a life insurance salesman desperate to sign up another client. I wouldn't give up until I closed the sale.

Al and I split the cost of the bus ticket to New Jersey. Living in the structured environment that his brother and wife provided, A began making a big turnaround. He started doing well in his new school.

It only took one ingredient to ruin the recipe for success: dependency. If A lived with his brother, where would his mother's welfare train go? As the brother attempted to change over the food stamps and other minor funds necessary for helping A, his mother refused to cooperate. A quickly ended up back in St. Louis with his mother. Soon A found his way to Juvenile Court.

Last I heard of A, he was in prison as an accessory to murder.

Decades ago, Newt Gingrich advocated taking some kids out of their homes and putting them in group homes, saying that they would be better off. There was an uproar in response to the idea, but maybe, for a kid like A, it wouldn't have been such a bad idea.

13

My Friend Tommy

The last time I saw Tommy, I had to carry him out of Globe and help him sit down in the alley. He wore many scars, scabs, and open wounds on his face from fights, brawls, and plain old street life. As I maneuvered him by the arm, Tommy's stagger struck me as a sad reflection of his inability to navigate his own life.

He slid down onto the putty-colored cobblestone, and hissed and moaned. It made me remember the day I carried our greyhound, Abby, to the vet to be put to sleep — that same despondent look of "please, let me go."

Danny, a fixture in the St. Louis homeless scene, broke the news to me with a couple of tears dribbling from his left eye. Tommy, my friend for over 18 years, had died behind a small package liquor store in a remote part of downtown. Danny, a decorated but confused Vietnam vet, was Tommy's good friend. I shared the news with my father as he was chasing off some early morning imbibers. He responded that Tommy was better off. I knew he was right; a man can only endure so much suffering.

Still, Tommy will always have a special place in my heart. Though his life was filled with humiliation and suffering, I can't forget his contribution to Lift For Life and the kids who worked out there.

When I first met Tommy in the late '80s he had emerged from a maximum-security prison. He was clean cut with a bulging chest and biceps from working out his upper body every day in prison from the lack of anything better to do. He and his friends would visit Globe several times a day to buy cheap liquor to fuel their endless "happy hour". Then he would pass out, sometimes in surprising places — everywhere from the stalls in the bathroom to back in the warehouse on a stack of wooden four-by-four pallets. But as with most of the regulars who patronized Globe, I got to know Tommy fairly well and started giving him odd jobs to try to help him recover from his addiction. I would regularly send him to get me something to eat at the closest McDonald's and made sure that he could get something too. I didn't mind that most of the time, by the time he returned with the food, the fries were cold and limp.

I have witnessed so many losses to alcohol and drugs that I don't have enough tears to shed anymore. Homeless alcoholics know their fate — it's just a matter of when. Like soldiers going off to war, most know they won't be returning home.

Tommy helped me with a wide variety of projects. When I decided to open a gym for kids, he was among the small platoon of homeless men who, for a pocketful of cash and coins, helped clear the space. At the time, I barely had enough funds to open the gym and couldn't have managed without their help.

But Tommy's biggest contribution came when we were all sitting at the back of the store talking and eating burgers and fries. This tight-knit crew of rough, displaced men reminded me of cowboys sitting at a campfire on the foothills of a western mountain range eating jerky and drinking cheap whiskey. Despite their sarcastic barrage of comments, I knew that they understood the need to help kids. They, too, would have benefited from positive role models.

One man, Bob, whose fouled pants made me keep my distance, asked what I was going to call this place. I replied, "Probably Bulldog's Gym." But I added that I was open for ideas. Tommy offered, "Why don't you call it 'Lift For Life.'" I set down my half-eaten Quarter Pounder on the grimy table. He had my attention. "You're givin' kids a lift — they are lift'n for life," Tommy said proudly.

From that point on, I knew this was the name for my half-cocked adventure in helping kids. Sometimes, a name is everything; it says it all. And I owe that to Tommy.

Over the years, I have helped several homeless individuals, a few with great success. But for some reason Tommy could not turn it around. He had too much baggage. Maybe it was when he was in the Marines and came home from leave to accidentally catch his wife in bed with the next-door neighbor. Or immediately thereafter, when he robbed one of the two grocery stores in his small town of 2,000 without even wearing a ski mask to conceal his identity. Or when he was gang raped in prison during his first week as an 18-year-old inmate. Or perhaps the time when his sister told him she was unhappy and going to kill herself, and he said, "fine do it," and she did a few days later.

Tommy was simply bent on self-destruction. I figured it out when he came to the store with a multi-colored, bruised, puffed-up face that made him nearly unrecognizable. His friend Bob explained that you can't go into a bar at two in the morning and call people "niggers" without getting the shit kicked out of you.

I also remember the day at Globe when I heard several exchanges of curse words followed by a loud bang. I went to my dad's area to see what had happened, only to find Tommy skidaddling out of the store. Behind him, peanut butter oozed in globs from the 50% off greeting card rack. As I picked up the busted jar of Jiff, dad told me that Tommy had just called him a Jew and that I needed to "get him the hell out of here…NOW!" My dad, for all his kindness, transported a jar of peanut butter at the speed of a Katyusha rocket in response. At least it was the creamy.

Years ago I tried calling Tommy's brother and sister in the small town in Illinois where he grew up. I asked them to come and get Tommy, which they kindly did. They, too, tried to rehabilitate him, with some temporary success. He was very pleasant when they brought him back after a month — like a new man — but Tommy fell off the wagon way too many times.

Soon, I was calling his brother and sister again with the message they had been fearing most. How can you lose a brother at 52?

Only two weeks before his death, I saw Tommy limping down the street like a three-legged box turtle, a beaten man. Tommy was not more than 20 meters away when I hurriedly summoned our community relation's person.

"Do you see that man, the one that looks like a homeless person? Do you know what he is responsible for? He is the man who named Lift For Life.

She was stunned.

"That man?"

I said, "Yeah, I've known him for over 18 years, and he came up with the name. It's a great name isn't it?"

I don't even have a picture of him.

14

Heroes

When I started the gym in 1988, I barely had enough money to keep the doors open. I did pretty much every job imaginable: picking up the kids in my car, teaching them how to work out, cleaning up vomit, whatever needed doing. But as the years progressed, so did the organization. Along the path of success, there were donors, or as I call them, "investors," because they believed that investing in today's youth would help prevent criminals of tomorrow. These "investors" made Lift For Life what it is today.

One investor in particular, the St. Louis Variety Club, donates vans to not-for-profit agencies that need vehicles to transport program participants. The Variety Club turned us down the first two years that we applied for aid, but the following year we received approval. The donation of a van was a major turning point. The days of hauling kids in my beat-up Camaro were over. This one investment transformed the gym into a more accessible destination. The next step was to raise money for a driver. That way we could not only service the dozen or so kids who came regularly, but also admit their friends who had been pleading to come.

Around the time we received the van, several local newspapers ran stories that drew positive attention. One article told about my taking eight kids out of town to compete in a power lifting contest at the University of Missouri-Columbia for the Show Me State Games. It's one of the state competitions that highlights every sport imaginable from Wolksmarching to rodeo, horseshoe throwing to rhythmic gymnastics, anything and everything to book every hotel room and eatery and bolster a college town's economy over the long summer. A reader phoned the very morning that article appeared.

I shook off my first gut reaction: "Okay, buddy, that's very nice of you, but I gotta go back to work." I get compliments all the time, but rarely is there someone who is willing to get involved. The caller introduced himself as Larry Eisenkramer and went on to tell me that although he had never heard of Lift For Life prior to reading the newspaper article, he loved the idea of building self-esteem through working out. What was different this time was that this energetic, positive man wanted to help and help BIG.

After we ended our call, I turned the contact over to my wife, Carla, who was an expert at grooming relationships to an active level. Soon Larry offered to volunteer by serving on our board, which had been put together on a shoestring. He then pulled along his friends and business associates in a way that would propel Lift For Life to the next level. Within two days we received a generous contribution from his family.

In less than a year, Larry became our board president, nurturing the organization in some very important ways. He helped create a groundbreaking food extravaganza known as "The Taste of Clayton," which raised tens of thousands of dollars each year for Lift For Life and another local charity. It alone kept Lift For Life in operation through its most financially challenging times.

Years later, Larry's wife Joan, one of the nicest people I have ever met, was diagnosed with cancer and eventually succumbed to the illness. During that sad period, Larry moved on from Lift For Life.

After that, Larry's life continued to spiral downward. In 2001, he was found guilty of fraud in connection with the handling of some of his clients' funds and sentenced to prison. Although he was punished for his crime, some people thereafter would still make derisive comments about him.

I know that despite Larry's wrongdoing, if it wasn't for him, Lift For Life would not be around today and would not have saved so many innocent kids from becoming career criminals, addicts, or lifetime recipients in the welfare system. In the divine equation I feel that has to count for something.

Because we now had a passenger van from the St. Louis Variety Club and money from the Taste of Clayton, we were in a position to hire a driver. I knew that we needed someone who had the patience and stamina to work a part-time job with action-packed kids.

I knew a man who had a small confectionery in a rough part of town. The area that the store was in reminded me of a Wild West outpost. It was separated by a major highway with only two or three streets providing access. As you passed through the entryway to the confectionery, the wobbly, hinged-door would sway in several directions. This neighborhood was one of the roughest and toughest in the city with frequent shootings, and drugs sold on the street.

As long as the sun was out, I enjoyed visiting the store, seeing Mr. Willie Lewis, the proprietor, sitting behind a century-old glass case filled with a wide array of penny candy.

Mr. Lewis loved chatting with the neighborhood folk, occasionally harassing a 7-year-old kid who had six pennies but didn't know how many pieces of penny candy that would buy. It was also clear ya don't fuck with Mr. Lewis.

Over time I had observed that Mr. Lewis had a passion for kids to do right. I recognized as well that he could use some extra money and would enjoy transporting the kids to and from the gym after he closed at night. We agreed on a small hourly rate, and the next week Mr. Lewis was behind the wheel with the kids.

When word got out that our gym now had a van and the ride was free, kids started coming in droves from all over the city. When Mr. Lewis was finished picking up the kids, he sometimes would fire up a 10-buck barbecue pit on Washington Avenue. This was an acceptable practice where he lived, but not really in the commercial area where the gym was located. Even so, I wasn't too concerned. Nothing like a barbecue cookout and feeding hungry, aspiring Arnold Schwarzenegers with newly bulging biceps.

The kids responded to Mr. Lewis with the utmost respect. I don't know if it was because his demeanor commanded it, or if it had to do with the night we had a 12-kid brawl and he helped break it up by swinging a warped bumper pool cue. He swung the stick like one of the seven samurai to break up the fight. I doubted that he would ever have hit the kids, but looks can sometime be deceiving. The fight immediately ended and everyone knew his place in the food chain.

Mr. Lewis drove one of those big Cadillacs from the days when big meant BIG and gas was cheap. His Cadilllac rode like a steamship on a calm sea.

We took many out-of-town trips together, hauling the kids to compete in New Orleans, Charlotte, Virginia Beach. Along the way, he would share stories of his life.

He once told me how during the Korean War his unit got ambushed in the mountains. Apart from one other soldier, his entire platoon was wiped out. When he heard the Chinese coming, he jumped into a foxhole, pulled a dead soldier over his body, and hid. The enemy soldiers walked to each and every body and pierced them with their bayonets. Unfortunately, Willie's midsection was the recipient of the razor sharp bayonet that pierced the dead soldier covering him.

Knowing he would die if he screamed, he passed out from the pain. Mr. Lewis said the next thing he remembered was waking up in a hospital already stitched up. From that day forward, Mr. Lewis walked with a limp. And from that day, he also refused government assistance.

Sometimes I think we were crazy. There were days we opened during a winter storm while the entire city was shut down. Mr. Lewis and I wanted to make sure kids had a place to go, and we went to extremes to show them we cared. The kids had two constants in their lives: one, the gym was almost always open; and two, Mr. Lewis would always come to their neighborhood, their front door, to make sure they were at the gym. When kids stopped coming or had a family issue that prevented them from attending, Mr. Lewis became a private eye, knocking on doors, talking to parents or grannies. He dug until he found out what the problem was and if there was any way he could help.

Mr. Lewis worked for the kids at Lift For Life for more than 16 years until his health began to decline. When that happened I was faced with the quandary of releasing him, which I couldn't bring myself to do. Helping the kids had become more important to Mr. Lewis than anything in the world. So instead, we figured out a way to have him still work at the gym, but not as a driver. That lasted for a while, but ultimately ill health prevailed, slowing him almost to a standstill behind his walker. Mr. Lewis finally had to retire.

We held a special retirement party for Mr. Lewis. Among those attending were many of the children — now adults — who Mr. Lewis used to ferry back and forth to the gym. It was a wonderful evening at one of the all-you-can-eat buffets. We established a scholarship award in his honor and presented him with a new suit for his remaining favorite activity: church. He would be the sharpest dressed person in the congregation.

At the party, we reminisced about the alligator boat tour we had taken in the deep Bayou of New Orleans, when an alligator almost jumped *into* the boat and us *out*! We recalled the amusement parks we'd visited and the time we took 38 high energy kids clear across the country in three vans to the coast of Virginia, while at every rest and gas stop there was a skirmish or two. None of this had been about the money for him. It had been about helping kids succeed.

I know I'll never forget Mr. Lewis. Eventually Mr. Lewis moved to a nursing home where, of all people, Eugene Starr resided. Alzheimer's and poor health kept him bedridden. Mr. Lewis eventually passed away in 2011.

Mr. Willie Lewis and Carla at his retirement party.

15

Tonka Toys

Sometimes I dwell too much on missed opportunities. I have seen many kids and adults with so much potential, yet due to time and other constraints in life, I haven't been able to help them as much as I would have desired.

Martez Robinson was a kid who made his life worth living, because he knew how to enjoy it. Anyone tagging along for the ride would enjoy it, too. Were he a little older, you'd want him to be your wingman at a singles party. Had he been the right age, he could have been Jim Carrey's sidekick on "In Living Color." But at this point, he was just 12 years old.

"America's Funniest People" was coming to St. Louis in the early 1990s, and Martez needed his shot. We made sure he got it. The only problem was that when Martez, Carla, and I arrived at the auditions late in the afternoon, everyone else was there to take their shot, too. By the time we got there, Martez was dead last in the audition line. In fact, so last that the weary talent scout stopped the auditions before Martez's turn arrived.

Imagine, Martez waiting in line like a child anticipating a ride at Disneyland, watching the person in front of him audition and coming up for his own turn, only to be told by the producer that was it for the day. We were flabbergasted. How dare they deflate Martez's dream?

Carla wouldn't stand for it. As she got increasingly assertive on Martez's behalf, the producer decided it would be easier to let Martez have a 40-second audition than to continue to listen to Carla's pleas. "Okay," he conceded, "but it's gonna be quick."

With that, Martez, four-feet, eight-inches tall and weighing all of about 78 pounds, took a chair in front and began inflating his stomach like Veruca Salt does in *Willy Wonka and the Chocolate Factory*, when she blows up like a blueberry balloon and is rolled off the set by the Oompa Loompas.

Martez' eyes began to retract as he went into the best imitation of childbirth I've ever seen from a skinny, 12-year-old black kid. From the size of his belly, he could have been giving birth to a baby rhino. He rubbed his egg-shaped belly and moaned. The cameraman, barely able to hold his composure, pushed his camera lens so close that it was millimeters away from Martez' protruding stomach.

But as I glanced at the producer, I saw that he was more interested in talking on his cell phone than watching the miracle of male birth. I knew Martez wouldn't be getting a callback.

After his delivery, Carla took Martez to Wendy's. He asked Carla if she thought he would get a callback. Knowing that the producer had been looking in the wrong direction, Carla was careful to promote Martez' self-esteem, regardless of whether or not he was picked for the show.

Weightlifting and competing were not a priority with Martez. Enjoying life and being a good friend topped his agenda. Martez was Vernon's first cousin and the two were also hang-out buddies with Gary. They attended the same grade school. Martez lived in the high-rise, crime ridden projects, like the many other kids that attended the gym.

Martez had finesse with a capital F., knowing how to be smooth, when to push and when to take his foot off the gas. He could make you laugh on the dullest of days and still to this day, I don't know what his mission was.

Occasionally I would let Martez work at Globe, but there were so many other kids who were closer to me and had first dibs. It didn't bother him one bit.

Several months after the big audition to nowhere, I was driving my car through a vacant downtown in the late afternoon. You could feel the eeriness. Back then, before downtown St. Louis experienced a rebirth, there was very little activity apart from the baseball, football and hockey games that brought in folks from the county.

Butted up next to Globe's warehouse store is the highway overpass leading to Illinois. Below the overpass were several crisscrosses of viaducts that resembled a crossword puzzle, and below those a parcel of vacant land. The land belonged to the 26-story federal building that sat next to it. Since business was booming for the government, officials decided to build more parking on the vacant lot for the federal workers.

I had just gotten off work at the store and was on my way to drop off Raymond, who lived in the projects not far from the store. We began the slow drive along the lengthy viaduct with our windows rolled down, because my air conditioner only worked every other half-moon, when out of nowhere Raymond shouted out, "Look Marshall!" I slowed the car still more while navigating to the side of the viaduct.

"What are you looking at?"

"Look man, down there; can't you see anything?" he said in an agitated voice.

I stuck my head out the window and squinted over the viaduct. I heard the faint rumble of a diesel engine, though, with an occasional sharp bang.

I peered further down the viaduct while almost coming to a complete stop and spotted a cloud of dust.. Then, as the wind carried the dirt away, my eyes connected with a bright yellow bulldozer.

And there, lo and behold, a small, light brown Afro protruded through the cloud of dirt. I pushed my glasses higher up my long nose to get a better view and saw young Martez riding this dinosaur-sized bulldozer.

I have never seen anyone more focused than Martez. He pulled the lever to lower the bucket and scraped up several tons of gravel from one end of the lot before unloading it at the other end, while occasionally zig-

Martez and I discuss a workout in the early '90s.

zagging the machine in a counterclockwise direction for the sake of stirring up more clouds of dust, and, yes, sometimes hitting the column that supported the six-lane highway above.

As I held my breath in astonishment, I pondered whether I should be proud of Martez for helping to finish this no-end-in-sight-slow-moving, federally funded improvement project. Some part of me felt like a father at a peewee football game watching Martez's audacious plays from the bleachers.

As Raymond and I laughed in amazement, I thought about what a sheltered life I'd had growing up. My mom always wanted to know where I was. Despite having lots of games and toys, I'd never gotten to take my Tonka Toys or Matchbox cars for a ride. But Martez sure did.

As the security guards and off-duty police officers closed in and surrounded Martez, he leaped off the bulldozer while it was running full-steam ahead, dashed across the bow, and then zipped across the railroad tracks to hide in the projects. The guards were no match for him.

Several days later I scolded Martez for his inappropriate behavior, even while quietly appreciating his strong zest for life.

Martez currently resides in Jefferson City, Mo. He is doing well, working and spending time mentoring kids and young adults.

16

Vernon

You may remember Vernon Russell, the 15-year-old that I mentioned in the prologue. The 15-year-old that had gotten into so much trouble. We had met just a few years earlier in 1989 or '90 through Raymond and Raymond's younger brother, Gary Moore.

One morning back then, I asked Vernon and Gary what they were doing at the store so early. The two weren't brothers, but I called them "twins," because they did everything in tandem like a pair of ballroom dancers.

Vernon and Gary were smart 12-year-olds. Both had beanstalk syndrome, like most kids their age. Every time I saw them, they had grown several centimeters. When their muscles started blossoming, they became best friends with the mirror. Almost all workouts came with a pose down. Most of the time it was funny and we all shook our heads.

Both became strong and won many medals and ribbons. They enjoyed the taste of lifting competitions and would do whatever it took to beat their opponents.

Gary was an expert in the field of psychology. He would push me as well as everyone else in his life a step beyond sanity. He knew just what buttons to push to get me either to explode or yell and would then watch my face flush. He knew how to deliver his punch line at the right time. It took me a half a year to figure out how to counter his moves.

While Gary was causing chaos, Vernon was more strategic. He realized that being respectful and occasionally helping out at the gym or the store earned him brownie points that brought food or candy.

"So what are you doing here?" I asked a second time, knowing something was up. If just the two of them showed up at the store, they knew their chances of getting a snack increased, since I wouldn't be able to give ten kids each a candy bar. "We got out early. It's parent-teacher conferences," they responded together with mini-giggles.

"Oh, that's good," I replied, "Are your moms going?"

"My mom's not going — she don't care. She's too busy," Vernon said sounding as if he had been let down. I had met Vernon's mother and knew she was a good person. But seeing how Vernon was doing in school was not a high priority. Holding down a job and single-handedly managing a family of several kids was draining, especially with a limited income.

"Let's close the gym a little early, and I'll go for both of you. I'd like to see how you guys are doing."

They conveniently added, "Let's go out to eat, too." The "twins" were never shy about expressing what they wanted. Perhaps this was the way they had to be to get by in life, but I didn't mind. Their company was always amusing.

The three of us drove to their school, which was near the public high rise apartments where they lived. As we walked in the dimly lit building, I noticed the walls were nearly bare except for some "Stay in School" and "Don't Do Drugs" posters and a smattering of student art.

Vernon and Gary introduced me to their teacher. The teacher looked puzzled. I affirmed that I had come as their coach, and the teacher then showed me their report cards while explaining the curriculum. Since there were no other parents attending, she decided to give me a more lengthy explanation.

"Oh, Vernon is a great kid. He is so nice and such a good student," the teacher shared happily. Sitting next to me, I think Vernon was excited that I would take the time to see how he was doing in school.

I listened to the teacher for 10 minutes or so, while I mentally drifted slightly out of the meeting, thinking to myself, "Where in the world are all the other parents? This school has at least a couple of hundred students, and maybe a dozen parents are in the entire building! What is wrong with this picture?"

It's funny the things we remember, while other memories come and go. Though it was 17 or 18 years ago, every time I pass near that school, I am reminded of that unsettling occasion.

My other memory of Vernon comes on the day he turned 13 when we held a celebration, as we do for all kids, at the gym. These are always happy events, but Vernon's birthday celebration went south right after we sang the birthday song.

We cut the cake and started passing it out, only to see steam come from Vernon's face. He was outraged that my poor wife, only trying to do the right thing, purchased a chocolate cake instead of vanilla. We had no idea that Vernon preferred vanilla to chocolate.

We felt terrible about it, especially knowing that when he entered the door to his mom's government subsidized apartment, no birthday treats would be awaiting him there. Vernon had been looking forward to this party. His disappointment revealed how raw his emotions were. Unfortunately, he was too young to understand that we truly were there for him.

As time went on, I thought Vernon and his clique were on the right path. It's so tough to gauge. We went to many out-of-town competitions, and Vernon was among those excelling. But you can only do so much without completely removing an impressionable teen from a nasty environment. Vernon and his friends slowly started moving into the fast lane, and neither I, nor any other stabilizing factors, would prevail.

Early on the morning after I found Vernon scared and bleeding on the stairs, I tried to rectify things. While eating my cereal, I flipped through

Vernon pumps iron on Washington Avenue.

the *St. Louis Post-Dispatch*, like I normally do every morning, and came across a photo of Vernon's "dude" in handcuffs next to the smashed car they had stolen. I realized that I needed to talk to Vernon's mother and tell her what had happened, and do it soon.

The sun had not yet peeked beyond the city's skyline when I knocked on her door. I guessed that I would be waking her up. I was a little uneasy in that neighborhood, but more than that, I was oddly concerned with not wanting to inconvenience her. The uncomfortable feeling reminded me of when I was nine or 10 years old and used to go door-to-door selling overproduced tomatoes and cucumbers from my dad's garden, or offering my unwanted services to rake neighbors' leafless yards.

Suddenly, the door opened.

Without hesitation, I held the newspaper in front of her sleepy face. "Look, Mrs. Russell, you have got to talk to your son! PUNISH HIM — he can't do this kind of stuff!"

"Oh, I'm goin' to talk to him," she said sleepily, while rubbing her arm and looking at the paper.

"Vernon was the other person who got out of the car and ran from the cops!" I insisted.

She repeated that she would do something, and I apologized for waking her up.

When I got to work, I phoned Vernon's older brother, with whom I had a passing relationship based on our having discussed Vernon and his lifestyle. The brother held down two jobs, two, because one job just doesn't earn enough to make it.

"Hey, you need to talk to your brother, can you spend more time with him; he is out of control," I ranted.

"I'll try," he responded wearily.

So who can we blame? Who is supposed to fix this turbulence before it gets too windy? The mother, the brother, or perhaps the police? The mother with limited time and resources, the brother holding down two jobs, or me, giving him brief moments of success that were not powerful enough to counter balance the magnet of street life?

After a while, Vernon replaced going to the gym with living the life of the streets. I occasionally saw him in the years that followed. The hard-earned muscles he achieved in his early teens had disappeared. He was just another slim, cheap wooden toothpick in a box of 500; the fast life, drugs and alcohol were taking their toll.

Shortly before Vernon's 19th birthday, one of his friends came to Globe

Drug and delivered the news: "Vernon got shot last night; he got killed."

I went limp inside.

I asked what had happened, and the friend replied it was over a blunt cigar. Later someone said the killing had something to do with drugs or money.

At the standing-room-only service, Vernon's friends sang and everyone cried. The pastor spoke pointedly about street life in general and Vernon in particular. His mother, seeming to take umbrage, got up, turned abruptly, and walked out of the chapel in the middle of the service.

I thought back to the night she hadn't been available to meet with Vernon's teacher and wondered if things would have been different. Would it have been different if I had called the police when I found Vernon on the stairs?

While it was distressing seeing Vernon's mother walk out of the funeral, perhaps other street kids present who heard the pastor's hard words realized that there is more than one path in life.

If I had that chance to put another coin in the slot machine and try my luck again, I know what I would do; but life has no replays.

Vernon's mother did not have much time to reflect on her "what-ifs." She died six months after Vernon's funeral.

17

If The Shoe Fits

At the time I started the gym, I was working at Globe and operating a small video game business. I would supply small "mom and pop" confectioneries with candy, soda, and chips. If room in their stores permitted, I would give them a couple of video arcade games and split the proceeds with them.

At first the arcade games did well, but then home versions of video games began appearing and that put me out of business. Gone were the days of kids hanging out at the local candy store; instead, they would lie around on their couches, gain weight, and play the same violent game over and over until it was imprinted in their brains.

When the few games I had left needed repairs, I tried to fix them myself to save money. If a quarter was jammed, or if some genius slid a wooden grape popsicle stick down the coin slot, I had to remove it carefully, like taking out tonsils.

There was one store in particular that still had several games of mine. You could buy anything and everything at that store, from a pound of bologna to a $5 sandwich bag of marijuana cut with cheap spices. The owner was even known to sell a can or two of beer without a liquor license. Whenever I came to take an order, the owner chatted and shared information that, frankly, I would rather not have had. For instance, he would reveal that a utility company had stored 55 gallon drums marked "Danger" in the vacant building attached to the store.

I was phoned repeatedly to repair the games, mostly on Friday and Saturday nights, but I didn't care because the location was a big money maker. Many of the kids who came to the gym also hung out at this store. Edward Culpepper was a fixture there and at the gym. He had been one of our first kids at Lift For Life. Whenever I had to tell Edward the gym would be closed for the day, it was like telling him he wasn't getting a present for

Christmas.

Since Edward lived in the projects across the street from the store, he was available to help me fix the games. He had a special knack for repairing things, a real pro at fitting A into slot C.

As we worked, there was always a particular 9-year-old kid, Michael, hovering around us like a half-full helium balloon. I would have one eye watching what I was doing so I wouldn't get an electrical shock from one of the bumpers, and the other eye focused on this kid.

I asked the boy repeatedly what he wanted. No response. He would just step back and wait several minutes before coming back like a swinging door to watch us. I asked Edward whether he thought this kid would want to come to the gym, and Edward replied, "You don't want that kid comin'; he's a bad kid, always gettin' on people's nerves."

But to me the boy just seemed curious, and the kids I like best are the curious ones who seem motivated to do something, whatever that something might be. So after I finished repairing the machine and brushing the greasy grit off my hands, I told Michael about the gym and asked if he wanted to come. He was as delighted as if he had received two toys instead of one in a McDonald's Happy Meal.

I told him to meet us at Globe Drug after school and to make sure he got permission from his mother. Edward shook his head slowly back and forth in disgust. I asked what was wrong, but he didn't respond. Perhaps Edward thought that he would receive less attention from me.

On Michael's inaugural day, he met up with the platoon of muscle builders at Globe. You could see his hesitation mixed with several gallons of excitement. The group jammed into my Camaro and since Michael was the youngest, he was squished and maneuvered into a dubious yoga pose against all respect for the human body. But he didn't care, because he had a place to go. As the older kids shoveled verbal abuse on Michael, I told them to leave him alone, while distractedly listening to my muffler scrape clean the century old cobblestone pavement on our way to the gym.

My routine was to train the older kids first. We did our usual grueling workout as Michael watched eagerly. After an hour, I spent some time showing Michael the basics of lifting weights. I didn't realize how strong he was until I handed him the beginner bars and noticed that it didn't faze him one bit. This was at a time when Arnold Schwarzenegger movies were the hottest tickets at the movies theaters. Every kid wanted a ripped body like Arnold's. Thanks to him, the kids had a role model and a reason to be healthy and work out.

Although I was impressed with Michael's strength, I also noticed the assortment of quarter and half-dollar sized holes in the soles of his shoes that were nearly twice the size of his foot.

I wondered whether the shoes were a fluke, if he just hadn't been able to find his own shoes that morning. After several days of coming to the gym, it became clear that these were in fact Michael's only shoes. During a workout one day, while he was doing a set of bench presses, I asked a barefooted Michael where his shoes were. He explained that he'd removed them because there were holes in the soles, and when it was rainy, as it was that day, his socks and feet got wet.

I asked when he was going to get a new pair. He replied that his mother was going to get him shoes when she got her 'check.' Having some knowledge of government assistance, I understood that would be several weeks away, because the first of the month just passed. Food would come first, so shoes might not even make the cut that month.

Then, between repetitions of lateral pulls, I contemplated which bothered me more: having President Ronald Reagan's administration deny there was an AIDS epidemic, having a squirrel nibble on my nearly ripe garden tomatoes, or having a nine-year-old-kid go through his formative years wearing clown shoes. Since I could only make an impact on one of these problems, I told Michael to come to my dad's store after school the next day, and we would buy a new pair of shoes. The condition was that he promise to sweep the gym for two weeks to pay me back. He agreed instantly.

Michael showed up early – as if he had a half day of school while the entire district of 40,000 other students had to attend a full day. I didn't care. If new shoes would make Michael feel good about himself, I knew that this would help him over the long haul.

When Globe closed for the evening, an eager Michael and I took off to the closest Target. We arrived at the shoe aisle, and Michael began to scan the merchandise. Within minutes he narrowed his choices. I don't think he did this intentionally, but he managed to pick shoes that were only a fraction smaller than those he had been wearing. He had unconsciously become accustomed to the too-large size. I told Michael to take off his shoe, and we measured his foot. Soon he understood what shoe size he needed.

Looking down the aisle for the correct shoe size, he selected the most board-stiff running shoe ever manufactured. He was thrilled with them.

As he laced them both up and did a short walk about down the shoe aisle, I was satisfied that he would be safe from ridicule for a while.

Michael smiled as he turned back and said confidently "Yeah, these fit good." Still, what good is a sandwich without crisp lettuce and a juicy, ripe tomato? So I told Michael to grab a sack of white tube socks also, and we went off to pay.

The following day I took the gym kids to the movies. I sat next to Edward, while Michael and the other kids filled the remainder of the seats down one row of an otherwise empty theater. For some strange reason, smack in the middle of the movie, Edward leaned over and told Michael, "You better thank Marshall for buyin you those shoes!"

Michael repeated to me, "Thanks for buyin me these shoes," as he stretched his legs and placed his shoes comfortably on the back of the empty seat in front of him.

Edward then added to me, "My momma said thanks, too."

"I don't get it. You mean you guys are brothers?" I asked, puzzled.

"Yeah," said Edward, "but he still gets on people's nerves."

Michael continued to come to the gym for another ten years. He turned out to be one of the most decorated weightlifters ever to attend Lift For Life Gym, traveling all over the country to compete. During that time, he worked at Globe for extra pocket money. At times, he would sneak into the warehouse to drive the forklift down the long aisles. I got a tongue

Michael adds another kilo. *Photo by Steve Weintraub.*

lashing from my uncle for having him hang around and getting caught driving the forklift.

Years later, when Michael came back to visit as an adult, he recounted how much the gym had meant to him. And, by the way, he just so happened to be a fork lift operator for a big company.

Michael makes his lift at an inter-gym contest.

18

GUYS AND DOLLS

I arrived at Globe a little earlier than I liked on this particular morning. Making the trek up the long, metal stairs to the store from the parking garage, 47 steps in all, was a workout by itself. I reached the antique, steel door at the top and took a low, deep breath the way my former yoga teacher always preached, "Breathe from the bottom of your lungs, slowly filling your lungs to the top."

With my heart pounding against my sternum, I couldn't fool myself into believing I was in good shape. When I reached my chair, the light on my answering machine was blinking red almost as fast as my heart was pumping. I pressed the button and heard a familiar voice come from the quarter-sized speaker.

"Marshall, man, can't you send me some money?" the message started abruptly. "I'm locked up, man, you should help me, send me some money. It's O, man, pick up the phone, man, if you's is there." A long pause and then, "Marshall mannnn…!" click.

I looked down in disgust and disappointment knowing that all of this could have been prevented. Another young adult on the path to becoming a career criminal. Another wasted $25,000 a year to warehouse someone.

As I walked along the long narrow aisles of whatnots, I reflected on my memories of O I glanced at the bathroom, remembering the times O would skip school and sneak into the store's bathroom. He would sit on one of the thrones to read X-rated, porn magazines that he'd stolen from the snack shop that was operated by a sight-impaired man in the nearby federal building.

I told him it wasn't right, but he insisted that the "adult peoples that worked there in that government building ripped that man off all the time, walking out with stuff," and "Heck, they are gett'n paid! Stealing from a blind man!" he said.

He had shaken his head indignantly. Go figure. He was irate that working adults were stealing from this shopkeeper, but that had made it okay for him to steal a couple of porn magazines.

You could make some allowances for O given his temperament. He was more than likely born to a crack and alcohol-addicted mother.

When O first started coming to the gym, he was always moving at a dragonfly's pace, hyper and jittery. You could get nervous just looking at him.

His friend, Terry, who used to live a floor below O in the projects, told me a bit about his upbringing.

"Man, his mother would beat him so much you could hear the walls shake. My momma had to call in on her (to child protective services) a few times," he said. "She would beat O so bad, that I felt bad."

"That would explain all the scars on his face?" I asked Terry.

"Marshall, she even used an iron," Terry said more softly. "The child people came, took 'em away for a little, but brought 'em back a few days later."

I felt bad that I couldn't have done more to turn back the hands of time. But you can only do so much.

Through the years, O had enjoyed lifting weights when he came to the gym. He was a specialist in power workouts. He would come in and do a massive amount of bench presses and curls in as little as fifteen minutes. He got a quick pump-up, similar to getting a quick high. His mini-workouts were focused on his chest and arms only, completely neglecting the rest of his body. After he would do his power workout, he would dart out and go hang out at Union Station.

One time, while finishing his abbreviated workout and flexing his biceps in the mirror with a Grinch-like grin, he said, "Marshall, girls really like muscles!" I knew exactly what he meant as he flexed his pecs and biceps one more time in the mirror to make sure they were still there.

But O's world soon closed in on him. He smoked dope, dropped out school, engaged in petty theft and spent more and more time behind bars.

Later that day, I listened to the message on the recorder one last time. Then I erased it. That is what we do in life. We erase what we have no use for, who we don't want to deal with.

O's sister J was the complete opposite. J and her friend Danielle were among the first girls to come to the gym. They didn't care too much for working out with weights, but enjoyed our social excursions: going to movies, restaurants, and the amusement park.

Both attended school every day and were always doing something positive with their lives. They comprehended that their ticket out was to stay in school.

J and her friend wanted to work, but I already had a jam-packed group of kids working in the store and had nothing to offer.

But the two found a way. My family's store sold discount candy bars, some large enough to feed a family of four. Customers would resell them for fundraising events. The girls, along with O, resold them for their own profit, hitting up the average Joe on a downtown street. Danielle and J could sell to anyone.

O was very tactical and taught the girls where the best places were to hang out and wait. He had the smarts to figure out where the large downtown companies were located and when they would release their employees. Southwestern Bell was one of his hot spots. The surge of people exiting the 20 plus-story building was a gold mine for the kids.

They were successful to a fault. One day a customer at the store told me he happily gave a kid a five-dollar bill because he said he was raising money for Lift For Life Gym. I knew who that had to be. Later I confronted O and told him that it wasn't right to say he was selling candy bars for our charity while pocketing all the money.

There did come an occasion, though, when I was able to

O flexes his muscles after a workout.

hire the girls to do a job for me. One of my best friends was having a small party that night for his three-year-old daughter, and I needed a present. So I had the two girls run an errand for me.

I didn't mind that I would be paying double for the gift, the cost of a doll plus the charge for the errand to a downtown mall.

I asked them to get a doll for a 3-year-old for no more than 15 dollars. The two were excited to go on this mission, and asked if they could also get something to eat at McDonald's. I replied, "No problem," and gave them a few extra bucks for the dollar menu.

I knew that the two would take more time than allotted, because they had to look in every store whether they sold dolls or not. It was what my sisters would have done at that age. Still, the hours passed, and I wondered what could possibly be taking so long. Closing time was approaching, and I grew concerned that they wouldn't be back.

I had looked out the window a dozen or so times before they finally slid inside the door, a fraction before closing time. They proclaimed proudly that they had found a doll as they handed me the bag. I paid each girl $8 and then started to pull the doll out of the bag.

I was startled by the discrepancy between what I thought I was getting and what was actually in my hand. I had assumed that the doll I would be giving to my Jewish friend's daughter in the burbs was going to be your standard, Caucasian type, but instead it was the African-American version.

The two girls were so pleased that they had found a great gift; but, in my mind, something completely different was going on. How could I give my friend's kid a black doll? Wouldn't they think it odd? So, after work and without telling J and Danielle, I returned the doll and traded it in for the Caucasian version.

To this day, I wish I had kept it and given it to their daughter. A doll is a doll, isn't it? What does a child know about skin color, unless we as adults lead them to a conclusion?

Years later, when my wife and I had two daughters, they would have an array of dolls, Asian, Hispanic, and of course African-American. They play happily with all of them.

O is searching for a steady job. J is working with children in juvenille detention. I've lost contact with Danielle.

19

A Diamond In The Rough

Good news can be like a flower in a weed garden, something positive blooming in the mass of negatives that bombard us daily. When a television news story about the gym appeared, I was inundated with calls congratulating me about the work we were doing.

But one call in particular stood out. It was from a high school freshman who managed to figure out how to get in touch with me though we didn't have a phone listing. To track us down, he called the television station, which passed him on to the reporter, Malcolm Briggs of KSDK.

The high school freshman wanted to know how much it would cost to attend the gym. "It's free," I replied. He asked if he could come down with his mom to see the place, and I answered, without a second of hesitation, "Sure." I didn't think much of it and doubted that he would show.

He proved me wrong, arriving the next day, with the reliability of a wave hitting a beach.

The gym at this point looked like the place where Rocky Balboa worked out with Burgess Meredith in the first Rocky movie. Paint was peeling off the wall. Discolored Astroturf covered not quite all of of the gym floor. Cheap extension cords powered the lighting fixtures that provided a dim glow. All this contrasted crazily with a wide variety of brand new, muscle-building equipment, enough to pump up a small platoon of bodybuilders.

What we lacked in looks we made up for with boundless energy.

I greeted Solomon Alexander and his mother with an outstretched hand. Raw enthusiasm was visible in Solomon's eyes. To Solomon, this "funkified" two-bit gym was all he needed.

Solomon brought back memories of when I wanted to join a gym, but found that the proprietors wouldn't allow kids. I felt vindicated in welcoming Solomon to this bodybuilding party in the hood.

We started building our connection with my stock question about what high school he attended. When he mentioned my alma mater, Ladue, I knew our relationship would build. It turned out that he had the same counselor, Dr. Richard Eaton, the same favorite coaches like Phil Brusca, who believed in every athlete regardless of ability and teachers like William Heyde. Though Solomon lived in a part of the city known for frequent shootings, he attended a high school in the county, one of the wealthiest districts in Missouri. He was one of the desegregation students, or the "deseg kids," as we called them.

I soon realized Solomon was something special. During our conversation, he stated, "This is the kind of place I've been looking for; I need a place like this."

Solomon asked if we provided transportation. I responded that my dilapidated Camaro was already overflowing with an assortment of bodies and that if he wanted to come he would have to figure out how to make it down to the gym on his own. I thought that he might come once or twice a week, but instead he came as often as we were open, no matter the weather.

Each day, Solomon worked out long and hard, more so than any other kid. On some days, I practically had to force him to stop so we could close the gym. While most of the kids tended to work out for a half hour and then go play and socialize, Sol would be hard at it. He was a man on a mission.

When I first started the gym, I placed a focus on building muscles and potentially competing in bodybuilding contests. But I found there was rampant cheating among competitors using steroids. Instead I aimed our attention on power lifting. The playing field was fair and the odds of some of our kids winning medals was high.

As summer approached, I entered my small platoon in the Show Me State Games, in Columbia, Mo. The kids trained hard. We rented a van, and took off to compete. Apart from the joy they took in competition, I knew it would be a terrific life lesson for them. They would get away from their two-neighborhood block mentality, which led most of them to believe that the rest of the world was exactly like theirs.

We stayed in a university dormitory. This was great because the kids got to see what campus life was like and it gave them a chance to think about setting their sights on a college education.

The Show Me State Games are a small, mini-sports festival with everything from track and field to trap shooting.

The power lifting competition was held in a small, out-dated, stuffy middle school gym. I could tell we were in for real treat when at the 7 a.m. weigh-in, you could feel the heat pulsating from the masonry blocks.

The kids took their turns weighing in. Some of them had issues with undressing and stepping on the scale in front of other males. But they followed through after I explained that everyone had to do it to compete.

For the next six hours, I felt like I was trapped inside a Native American sweat box in South Dakota in late August. But I didn't care; the kids were having such a good time lifting and cheering each other on — what more could anyone ask?

Most rewarding was seeing our little team become united in cheering and pumping each other up for each participant's turn in the competition. Kids who in the past had denigrated one another with volleys of insults, on this day supported and respected one another.

As we cheered each other on, I saw Solomon's mother and older sister walk into the gym and head toward our little outpost on the bleachers. Solomon was elated that his mother and sister drove more than two hours in a battered car to see him compete in a hot, smoldering gym in the middle of nowhere.

That afternoon Solomon was going against another kid who had a better trainer, more experience, and the latest in power lifting apparel. Sol and his rival kept going back and forth for the lead.

The lifters were separated by only 2.5 pounds and the competition came down to the last lift. The other athlete went out on the platform and lifted an ungodly amount of weight, propelling him so far ahead it forced Solomon to make a choice. Sol could lift a weight that he did time and time again in practice and place a solid second, or he could lay it all on the line and lift a weight that he had never tried.

Although I generally make the final decision after I confer with the athlete, I will usually allow the athlete in a do-or-die situation to make the choice and take responsibility. So much value is added when a young person can take ownership of the decision. First, though, I make sure the athlete understands the situation, for example: "If you don't make this you'll get third, but if you make it you take home first. Whatever you decide, I'm behind you. Your finishing position doesn't mean anything; I just want you to do your best. What's important is that *you* know you did your best."

You can see the gears in the kids' brains churning with a decision that is out of their norm. For that one moment, they are out of the survival mode of: what am I going to do for school clothes tomorrow; or, how will my mom cover the light bill that she is so stressed out about; or, it's the end of the month, we're out of food stamps, and there's no food in the house — what am I going to eat?

It all disappears for a moment in pleasant distraction. Some choose to stick with the weight they know they can comfortably lift; others like to go for it, because they know in life opportunity may only knock once.

After the other competitor succeeded in his lift, Solomon and I huddled quickly calculating what weight he would need to lift successfully in order to win the oversized, first-place medallion.

I asked Solomon what he wanted to do, and he paused to ponder the options, which were pretty slim. Either you do it, or you don't. He chose to go for it.

I approached the scorekeeper to tell him what Solomon's final attempt would be and watched as he wrote it down. Nudging his egg-shaped glasses away from his face in disbelief, he gave a brisk scratch to his stubby crew cut. "That's a big increase! Are you sure?"

I went back, gave Sol my final words of encouragement, and watched him on his way to the platform. He chalked up his hands, walked slowly to the bar, and bent over and grabbed it like he was going to wring a chicken's neck for his family's Sunday dinner. Solomon took several deep breaths. Then he began to drag the weight slowly up his shins.

He started to struggle at the halfway point. I watched while his head flushed dark as a bloody Mary. The blood vessels below his short afro were now visible and began to bulge like a twisted garden hose suffering to get the water out.

Closer, closer he came to a full stance. His body was shaking so, I was tempted to tell him to let it down, otherwise he might become best friends with a chiropractor. But the only thing out of my mouth, out of his teammates' mouths, and more importantly — out of his mother and sister's mouths — were cheers as Solomon gained full stance with over 450 pounds in his hands. He shook like a leafless tree in a Kansas tornado.

The head judge motioned to put the weight down and signaled a good lift. We all erupted in joy, but Solomon's smile surpassed that.

As we gave each other high fives Solomon approached his mother for a good mother-son, deep hug. We congratulated the other lifter and wished him well.

After the award ceremony, we headed off to a victory feast at a fast food restaurant, where we took advantage of the special $2 meals.

All the kids were eating together except Solomon, who was sitting at a table alone, savoring his moment. I asked him how he was doing and congratulated him on a job well done.

He replied, "Marshall?"

"Yes?"

"Thanks," he said simply.

"For what?" I asked.

"Just thanks for all you do for these kids," he replied softly as he took a sip from his soda.

It's a compliment that I will savor for the rest of my life.

THE ROAD BENDS

Solomon continued to come to the gym for workouts. But, as he grew older and became more involved with high school activities, I didn't see him as often. There came a time when he disappeared from the gym for several weeks, and I wondered if everything was okay. I finally received a call from the school counselor, Dr. Eaton. He told me that Solomon's mother had suddenly passed away. Solomon had grown up without a father. Now, at 17, he was motherless as well. His mother was the bedrock of Solomon's small family, the tanker ship that kept going regardless of setbacks, but now she was gone.

I got in touch with Solomon and passed on our condolences. I asked him to please let Carla and me know if there was anything that we could do though I wondered what any person could do. How could I help Solomon keep his head up and keep going?

But Solomon had determination, stamina, and tenacity, and he did keep going. Despite his tremendous loss, he managed to graduate high school, and subsequently enrolled at Rockhurst University in the Kansas City area. Once he left for college, we didn't keep in touch much. He would sometimes stop by the gym for a workout over the holiday break.

After four years, Solomon earned his bache-

Solomon, the athlete, at The Show Me Games.

lor's degree in marketing. No sooner had he returned home, than he called me up to say hi and to see how things were going at the gym. I'll never forget that call. I remember where I was standing, the time of day, which way I was facing, because at that moment I had a revelation. I realized that I needed help. I had so many kids coming to the gym, I could barely give any of them ample coaching time, let alone mentoring time.

Since Solomon had just arrived back in St. Louis, he didn't have a job yet. Nor had he even started looking for one. We agreed on an hourly rate. Solomon was thrilled to help out with the kids.

MATCHMAKER, MATCHMAKER MAKE ME A MATCH

My wife Carla wears many hats. Alongside her other roles, she handles Lift For Life's public relations. Carla cultivates a variety of media contacts, everything from small print papers in remote locations to media conglomerates. She has a special talent for pitching stories that get us interviews. Some interviews have been with early morning shows that only insomniacs would watch, whereas others have received prime-time coverage. Sometimes we've used volunteers standing outside television station windows with poster-board banners to promote a fundraiser. Regardless of the angle, it has worked.

On one occasion Carla booked a radio interview and asked Solomon to do the interview with her. On the ride over, it occurred to her that she had a friend there who was good-looking and single. She suggested that Solomon consider meeting her. He agreed. Upon arrival, Carla asked about her friend. The receptionist told her that Madelyn wasn't working there anymore, but she could tell Carla how to get in touch with her.

So like any good "yenta" matchmaker, Carla called Madelyn and suggested that she come down to the gym and check out all the good things Lift For Life was doing, and "Oh, by the way, you ought to meet this good-looking, single guy who's working down there helping Marshall and the kids." All in the same sentence.

Madelyn agreed, and the next week she came for a tour and just so happened to meet Solomon. They talked for a while, and it seemed that they were hitting it off. I didn't realize just how well until the next day, when Solomon told me he'd had a long conversation with her on the phone later that day. Within a year they were engaged.

When the wedding approached, Solomon gave me the highest honor — to be in his wedding party. I can't put into words how much that meant to me.

Madelyn and Solomon's wedding was at a small church, one of dozens, on the city's north side. This particular church was an old masonry structure. You could tell the church was used a lot because of the several small additions and updates to the building.

The place had a special feel to me. It was unusually warm and inviting. Being one of the only white people at the church wasn't uncomfortable at all. I was welcomed with open arms.

The service was wonderful, like all wedding ceremonies are. I stood there watching Solomon and Madelyn gazing at each other like any couple deeply in love, while at the same time glancing at my wife, who was dripping with joyful tears. I could only think what a "mitzvah" this moment was. If they hadn't met, what would their lives be like instead? What would Fiddler on the Roof be like without the actor Topol? Carla's amateur matchmaking skills had brought two people together who probably would never have met. I don't think anything in this world is greater than bringing two people together who fall in love.

Still, I couldn't help thinking how sad it was that Solomon's mother couldn't be a part of this joyous occasion. I'd had more opportunities to see many of Solomon's milestones than his mother. Solomon had made it safely out of one of the worst neighborhoods in St. Louis. He had put himself through college without parents, had a good job, and was taking the biggest step of his life in starting a family.

As I started to get choked up, I couldn't seem to get out of my mind that this church kind of looked like it could have been a synagogue back in the day. I knew there were many old synagogues from when this area was populated by a high percentage of Jews. I started to study the stained glass windows, which I noticed had elements of the Star of David and other biblical themes. The idea clicked in my mind that the upper seating area might have been where the women sat separated from the men.

The next day, without thinking too much of it, I told my Dad that I'd been in a church wedding and I thought the building might have been an old synagogue. I told him where it was, and he started to rattle off questions like a curious reporter. When Dad is interested, he generally asks the same question in several different ways. After my third time telling him where this church was and watching him visualize it in his mind, he told me that this was Bais Abraham, the synagogue he went to as a boy and where he had his bar mitzvah.

I thought to myself, how wild is that? Of all the two hundred or so churches in the city, of all the realm of possibilities in life, what are the chances of me, a white Jew, being in a wedding party in a predominantly black church on the north side that was the same place where my dad's family attended?

To top it off, I had been standing in the same place where my dad became a "man" in the Jewish tradition some 72 years before. Life is a circle.

Solomon continued with Lift For Life for many years. He also taught math at Lift For Life Academy, the charter school we opened. He later became Youth Sports Director at the St. Louis Sports Commission. Madelyn and Solomon now have a daughter.

Solomon, the coach, with two young athletes at the Junior Olympics.

20

Chain Reaction

Our group of young athletes proudly walked out of Logan Chiropractic College after another successful weightlifting competition. Chests were stuck out to display the pressed, recycled medals strapped around their necks. As we loaded the van, the kids shouted, "Please don't take us to MacDonald's! We done good — take us somewhere special!"

"Well," I thought to myself, "they did do their best. They behaved. What the hell, we don't have a ton of money, but they need to be rewarded for a job well done."

I quickly barked back, "We are going to Old Country…," but before I got out the word "Buffet," a wave of applause roared in my ears. The closest Old Country Buffet was a couple of miles away. It was sandwiched in an up-and-coming area of middle-and upper-class homes in a predominantly white neighborhood.

So, naturally, when we walked into the restaurant with 28 African-American kids, Charles, a Washington University junior who helped coach part-time, and me — a white Jewish man bringing up the rear — heads turned in the restaurant. "Thirty," I said cheerfully to the host.

"Let me rearrange the tables, and we will seat you soon."

I turned to Charles for help in explaining to the kids that this was a buffet, to take a little at a time instead of piling up a mound of food and not eating it all.

"I don't mind how many times you go back and forth, but please don't waste any food," I told the kids. "Remember, there are only two wings on a chicken, don't waste any; you might be able to let a chicken keep at least one wing." Most listened. Others smiled as their minds drifted to the aroma of tasty foods.

I love to take kids to new places. It is important for them to have experience outside their usual comfort level. The kids eyes lit up when they saw the buffet. Whoever designed the food stations at Old Country Buffet should get a design award; it's an amusement park for the taste buds.

The kids were wonderful, only taking exactly what they were going to eat. We were just pack'n' it in.

Pale green beans, creamy yams, crispy chicken wings, the whitest white rice, a collection of cakes and pastries to make a dietician cringe. Salads, pastas of every shape and form, honey-drenched ham, juicy roast beef… Food so sparkly and delectable that it looked fake, shining off the glowing, red-heat lamps. How could a child or a weight-conscious adult resist?

Now the key to the financial success of any buffet is to make sure there are plenty of starchy fillers. These will normally suppress an appetite quickly, but not with our kids. Not long after I tucked into my meal, I noticed a group of boys experimenting with liquids, salts, and imitation sugars and mixing them into their "bevys." They were guzzling them as if in a Gatorade commercial. I didn't pay much attention because they were behaving and keeping quiet.

I continued to shovel rice and corn mixture into my mouth, while watching Anthony pour several bags of sweetener into his cola and stirring gingerly. Minutes passed until Charles, my right-hand man from Washington University, told the sweetner gunslingers to wait outside.

Six boys left the restaurant with the others immediately following. I left a generous tip on the table while dashing a last nibble of angel food cake in my mouth and departed. Since I was still working in retail, I pondered what the heck a case of Sweet'N Low could have cost, because those six kids seemed to have devoured that much.

I didn't know the cost off-hand, but probably a lot less than the cost of the food flowing out of Anthony's hunched-back body out on the parking lot. He looked like a broken water main. As I saw poor Lil Anthony regain his posture, he smiled sweetly at me and loudly stated the obvious for everyone in the parking lot to hear: "Marshall, I just threw up, man." He said this with the sparkly eyes of a woman who has just given birth to triplets: the pure sigh of relief.

But no sooner had one athlete recovered, then 10-year-old, nearly 200-pound JR keeled over like a tanker truck on its side in the middle of the highway and spilled out his contents.

As an ice cream-jello-chicken-wing compost flowed forth from JR, Ebony, the cutest, most innocent 9-year-old ever, started exhausting herself too. Eight others relieved themselves as well.

I almost lost it myself. I had to walk away from the group. I could only remind myself to stay calm and breathe through my nose, just like what my orthodontist told me when he was jamming a full slab of quick-set concrete into my mouth.

The leader can never ever succumb to the problem. I struggled to regain my composure and slowly turned back to face the choir of heaves. JR, our Pillsbury Doughboy at four-foot ten-inches, 195 pounds, was collapsing into Charles' arms. Charles, barely able to hold up the rotund, slightly hysterical boy, looked to me for assistance. I grabbed one of JR's arms while Marlo, another 10-year-old, came up smiling and calmly stated, "I bet you guys weren't prepared for this."

Charles and I looked into each other's eyes without saying a word. Some things in life don't need words. Marlo was right. We were totally unprepared.

Like statisticians in a war room shouting out casualty reports, little 9-year-old TJ with the wild, afro version of Einstein's hair was providing up to the minute information on who was throwing up to whoever was listening. "OOW, Latasha just threw up her string bean casserole." He ran around the parking lot telling each herd of kids the latest: "Man, Marcus looks like he's goin' lose it next." At that point I intervened to halt the updates.

This was Sunday afternoon — peak dining time for hungry congregants.

Several cheerful church-goers pulled up to park but hurriedly retreated when they saw our kids regurgitating. Unfortunately, one family pulled up in a very nice, freshly waxed SUV and did park. As the wife in her fancy outfit stepped out onto the parking lot, she placed her left leather boot right in the middle of JR's starchy rice pudding. Unaware, she proceeded into the restaurant as if her only worry was when the sale was ending at Saks Fifth Avenue.

Tranquility finally prevailed. We boarded the vans for the 40-minute ride home.

As Albert Einstein once said, "Insanity is doing the same thing and expecting different results." Even so, three months later after another competition, we went to another all-you-can-eat buffet and didn't have a problem.

Sorry Mr. Einstein.

A group of proud (and hungry) athletes after a competition.

21

Roger That

The first kids that collected at Globe Drug in the late afternoon were lucky. They had an unfair advantage over the rest of the gym kids. They lived in the infamous Darst-Webbe Housing Projects, a five minute walk across the viaduct. They knew they would get the special "Marshall treatment": first dibs on seats in my car, and better yet, the 'fo sur' mentality that I would feed them a snack.

All the kids were gathered but we weren't quite ready to go. Roger, one of our homeless helpers, had left to go on errands five hours earlier and still hadn't returned. I paced in the front of the store as I peered out the window to the intersection below, hoping to see him. What did I think -- that at that precise moment Roger would magically appear in the street waiting for the light to turn green? I'm never that lucky.

I did an about face and hustled back to the rear of the store. Along the way, I grabbed the small chains that hung from the fluorescent light fixtures and pulled them one at a time, leaving a trail of lights out. I opened the green metal door to look down the long dingy stairway that led to the garage. No, Roger wasn't trekking up.

"Why you pacing, Marshall?" one of the kids said as chips grinded in his mouth. I didn't respond.

As with any typical end of the day, I helped my dad check out the registers, collect the money and close out the credit card machines. But this time, I slowed my stride to gain a few minutes in hopes that Roger would return. Still nothing. I corralled the kids and proceeded to the elevator with my dad, passing the green door again. This time, I didn't bother to open it.

I said goodbye to my dad and we climbed into the spare gym van. As we left the garage, one of the kids shouted, "Hey Marshall, where's your car?" I shook my head as I looked in the rear view mirror. Who is the fool?

The fool, or the fool who follows? Maybe I had put too much faith in my friendship with Roger.

It all started with a 69-cent sack of Bugler Rolling Tobacco. Every morning Roger would come to Globe to buy a pack. He was the first customer when we turned the key in the door. I don't know if it was because he didn't have anything to do, or the homeless shelter down the street kicked everyone out at 5:00 in the morning to go find work, or that we were five cents cheaper than the gas station down the street. Perhaps it was one of those multiple choice answers, D. All of the above.

At first, I didn't notice Roger because he bought his tobacco supply from Betty the front cashier. But it's like when you sit at a sushi bar, eventually someone says, "Can you please pass the soy sauce?" and then the conversation starts. Betty McNeese worked for Globe as long as I can remember. She started with us to earn for a few extra bucks when she was a newlywed and never left.

Betty had one of those enjoyable laughs that set her apart. Funny and sharp, she had the God-given knack of striking up a conversation with anyone that came in, regardless of their background. She was the type of employee that would have earned "employee of the month" if we had had such an award.

Betty began conversing with Roger. Soon enough, he had a chair made of boxes and a cozy place in the front of the store to roll his dried tobacco leaves and chat with Betty. Before Roger realized it, Betty had him taking the produce out of the coolers and doing other little tasks.

Roger was in his mid 60s, thin build, short white hair. At times it seemed like the synthetic hair you see on a Santa display. He kept himself immaculate given that he practically wore the same pants and shirt every day.

His last name was Scholer, German for scholar, and he was just that. He was one of the smartest guys I have ever known. He had a good career prior to something jolting his life and sending him to the streets. As I got to know him, he told me he was a former pilot for Ozark Airlines back in the 1970s.

Staffing at Globe was odd. I call it the Wal-mart factor. You can make money if you hire the minimum amount of minimum wage hourly employees. But you have to keep in mind that it only works if they all show up. When they don't, and you don't have enough staff to wait on customers, the result is a frustrated shopper and more work for the rest of us.

This opened the door for guys like Roger.

Over the months, I began to give Roger higher level jobs. It went well, although every so often he would gravitate to the famous bottle of spirits. The good thing was he seldom drank and it rarely disrupted the Globe's flow of commerce. Eventually, Roger made it on the "team" and was working around 30 hours a week.

During lunch breaks, I'd notice Roger running formulas on the calculator he always carried in his small canvas duffle bag. The calculator had more buttons than a centipede has legs. Occasionally I would ask him what he was doing. He said he couldn't fall asleep in the shelter, so he was testing a math equation he'd came up with in the middle of the night. If I asked him what the equation was he'd tell me. But to this day, I still can't comprehend what the dickens he was talking about.

In between, his favorite hobby was smoking multiple packs of cigarettes, accompanied by a horrendous cough and a swallow of mucus. Even his index finger couldn't escape the tobacco, with light brown stains tattooed from decades of smoking.

I loved seeing the expression on people's faces when they walked by Roger as he rolled his own smokes. They'd do a double take—"I can't believe this dude's rollin a joint in public!" Eventually Roger could afford pre-rolled cigarettes and the show was over.

One of the higher end jobs I gave Roger was letting him use my car for errands. He was efficient and could make a quick decision if a product he was picking up wasn't available. Best of all, he saved me time so I could focus on other things.

Roger was punctual. He had been doing errands in my car for months without a hitch. But this day was different. He had a huge list of stops that would take most of the day. I sent him on his way early in the morning. But by late afternoon, Roger was still out. I called several places that were on his list, no one had seen him.

I half-expected him to stroll into the gym while I was training the kids. The shelter he called home was a few blocks away. Wishful thinking. We closed the gym for the night, dropped the kids off and went home.

Since I am "a glass-half-full idiot," I came up with various scenarios. He had an extended cigarette break and dozed off after a satisfying smoke. Or perhaps he used my car to visit his adult son, whom he hadn't seen in years.

I entered the garage the next morning fully expecting Roger to be waiting for me. But my parking space was still vacant. The only thing between the grease covered lines was a fresh layer of warehouse dust.

It was a painful day. Every time the green metal door opened at the top of the stairs, I flicked my head back with a wish-filled glance. No Roger. Just the annoying slam-bang of an old iron door colliding into an equally old iron frame.

Word spread quickly among the employees that Roger had disappeared with my car. Even the gym kids knew about his famous disappearance.

I did the usual. I called the police department to see if my car had been impounded or if there had been an accident. I contacted tow companies. I called the hospitals to see if Roger was there. No sign of my car. No sign of my friend Roger. My poor hand-me-down black Camero with a single white door on the driver's side, where art thou?

I don't know why I didn't fill out a police report for my missing in action car. Perhaps because Roger came back a couple days later, early in the morning, raring to go, ready to work.

"What do you mean?" Roger asked after I inquired about what he did with my car.

"You haven't been here for a couple of days and you took my car for errands," I countered.

He looked at me and said in a soft-spoken voice, "car?"

I stood there for one of those long minutes you can have when you're at a party and someone tells you a joke. You pause for an uncomfortable minute -- not knowing if the joke is over or if you should laugh.

Not much surprises me anymore. I don't know if it's the lack of expectations I have of other people, or that Buddha thing that you just live in the moment and not try to fight what happens.

I explained to Roger that I had given him a bunch of errands. I tried to resurrect the conversation that we had prior to his leaving. Still, he had no recollection. It was like talking to someone who had been frozen in a capsule on the deep space mission from the movie *Alien*. He responded with typical Roger; pleasant, soft spoken, and gentle. I finally gave up after he replied that he just couldn't have taken the car, "You must be mistaken," he said.

In life, there are certain comments that require a necessary and sharp response. And there are other comments that require only silence to savor the moment.

LAWRENCE OF ARABIA

Lawrence Lewis was an only child. His mother, like mine, was over-protective. She kept his ass in church where he excelled in the choir.

But she also allowed him to come to the gym, after thoroughly checking us out of course.

Although Lawrence was never going to be the athlete on the top of the podium, he was one of those intelligent, thoughtful kids we knew was going to be a success. As they say, 'be somebody.'

When you see a kid cutting his neighbor's grass, or shoveling the sidewalk at the first half-inch of snow, you see a kid like Lawrence.

He worked out religiously at the gym and went on all our outings. While some kids wore me down with their constant shenanigans, Lawrence was a calm 13-year-old who blossomed in our program. He was quick to give a compliment and show his appreciation for all that Lift For Life did for kids.

After a number of years, Lawrence drifted from the gym. It's not unusual for the older high school kids to focus on getting a job, legally or otherwise, and only stop by occasionally.

So I was a bit surprised when Carla called me at work to tell me that Lawrence had left a message on our home answering machine.

"Hi Marshall, this is Lawrence Lewis. I happened to be walking by the hospitals in the Central West End and noticed a car that looked like yours.

'Lawrence of Arabia' (back row) with his teammates after a meet.

It has a bunch of parking tickets on it. I thought you might want to know. Looks like it's going to be towed any day."

A million thoughts flooded my brain at the same time. *Lawrence had the smarts to find my home number and call me. How considerate of him to let me know. What the fuck was Roger doing abandoning my car near the hospitals. And oh, how convenient, it's only a few blocks from my house.*

When I got home, I hustled up the street to retrieve my car. It was decorated with an assortment of parking tickets. Some a fresh bright yellow, others a dull tan, bleached from sitting in the sun for over a week. Mystery solved.

Roger continued to work for us for several more years. In the end, Roger's investment in the tobacco industry caught up with him and he succumbed to lung cancer.

As for Lawrence, he attended Webster University in Operatic Studies and traveled Europe in an opera company. He eventually moved back to St. Louis and is with the St. Louis Health Department working to fight AIDS.

I'm not sure I formally thanked Lawrence for finding my car. I bet I didn't even buy him a candy bar or a sack of chips.

22

It's A Small, Small World

"Marshall, I need $7," Little Walter Jackson said emphatically.

Everyone around the projects called him "Lil Walter," because he was so thin and innocent, he couldn't hurt a fly.

"Come on, please," he gently pleaded.

"What do you need the money for?"

"I need seven bucks for a haircut," he replied, as though negotiating a big contract for a fleet of used jets.

I remembered thinking that's a pretty good price. Heck, I pay $25 for my own wavy, tangled afro.

I knew that Walter was living in a Catholic Charities family shelter. His family had lost their opportunity to stay in the affordable projects, and perhaps a haircut was what was needed for Walter's equilibrium.

Walter was thin for his age, and no matter how many repetitions he did at the gym or how long his workouts, his size wouldn't change one bit. He

Carla helps Marcus with his homework. *Photo by Steve Weintraub.*

was a good kid, who never stood out. He was called peanut occasionally, too, because his skull was shaped that way.

Walter never took offense at the name. He loved going to contests and was proud no matter what place he finished. Sometimes he would walk around for days, if not weeks, with the medals he won. He was also a specialist in getting our lunch on Saturdays when we were working at Globe Drug. He was the fastest retriever of fast food, even if he sometimes got the order wrong.

As Walter was talking me out of the seven bucks, I couldn't help but notice that the shirt he was wearing looked like he had picked it up from the shelter's donated clothes closet: a mint condition, 1970-era Disneyland shirt.

It brought back warm memories of the time my family traveled to the West Coast to see our cousins and tour the amusement parks. My mom bought me a shirt just like it, and the chilling part was that I was approximately the same age as Walter. There are probably vintage collectors who would pay top dollar for the donated shirt on Walter's tiny back.

The shirt also brought to mind a visit years earlier with 40 of our kids — including Walter and his brothers Marcus and LeBaron — to the Six Flags amusement park in Eureka, Mo. What a dubious treat it was on a dreadfully hot, humid St. Louis summer with the kids determined to conquer every ride.

Within two-and-a-half minutes of entering the amusement park, I saw that the mandatory rule of hanging out together that I'd earlier imposed on the ride over was falling apart quicker than Jimmy Carter's re-election night defeat.

Without thinking it through, I told the kids to meet at the front gate at 6:30 p.m. All 40 acknowledged the plan but their senses were fixated on the bright lights and amusement park aroma. They broke off into clusters and went off down the black asphalt paths like so many pairs of Dorothy and Toto.

My wife had made it a point to emphasize to me the importance of keeping an eye or two on Marcus – Walter's older brother, who was then 9 years old. As we led a pack of younger kids to rides too small for a normal adult, we kept an eye on mid-sized Marcus. But then I had the ingenious idea to assign his older brother LeBaron to watch Marcus, and LeBaron assured us that he would. Since it was hot and my brain was only working at 10 percent capacity, I failed to realize that some rides had a 42 inch height requirement. Since the difference between LeBaron and Marcus was several years, it forced LeBaron to tell Marcus to wait for him at the exit while he rode the roller coasters. This left Marcus a wandering goat on a lonesome foothill.

When the day came to a close, and the group gathered at the front gate, I started counting kids and kept coming up short by one. No matter how many times I counted, how many ways I lined up the kids one child was still missing. It didn't take a genius to figure out who it was. Marcus.

We waited 15 minutes to see if he would show, and then organized a couple of search parties of teenagers to go out into the 200-plus acre park and bring our little soldier back. We searched every ride, every cotton candy vendor, every gift shop selling things that you questioned why you bought them the minute you woke up the very next day, but still no Marcus.

We backtracked on all the paths to each ride and combed every area. We went back to the front entrance several times to make sure he didn't surface there. After 90 minutes, we finally found Marcus at the bumper cars yearning for another ride.

"Marcus, do you know what time it is?" Carla scolded as she waved her Tony the Tiger wristwatch in Marcus' round, innocent face. "Do you KNOW what TIME it is?"

"Nope," he said, as he gazed at Tony's paws.

"Marcus, what time is it?"

"I don't know," he replied ever so softly. You could have heard cotton candy fall on the ground.

"Can you tell time Marcus?'" she asked gently.

'Nope," he responded. Carla and I looked at each other in amazement. My assumptions are challenged every day, but a 9-year-old not knowing how to tell time — this one really surprised us.

As we walked back, I gave Marcus my upbeat, positive speech about life and making it in the world. He smiled and said in a genuine voice, "Okay, Marshall." Just as if nothing had happened.

As Marcus aged, so did his need for finding things that entertained him. While driving one day to the projects to pick up kids for the gym, a car wiggled by me going the speed limit. At first it looked as if it didn't have a driver, but after I did a double take, I recognized the upper half of Marcus' head parallel with the middle of the steering wheel. One hand was on top of the wheel like he was in command, out for a cruise around the hood, the other arm was resting on the windowless door. Marcus, 11, at the time, was driving a stolen Pontiac Grand Am.

Seemed funny at the time, but Marcus' family suffered the consequences. Marcus, LeBaron and Walter's mother has always worked and wanted to have a good life.

Three strikes and you're out was the new rule in subsidized housing. If someone in your household repeatedly made waves as Marcus did, you were sent out into the wild blue streets. Just like a boot camp, one recruit errs and the entire platoon suffers. An innocent youngster like Walter pays the price.

About six months later, I was clicking the price gun on cans of whatnots and Marcus appeared out of nowhere, He started telling me that "if you don't behave, you don't get no haircut.

"Ya don't get no TV time, neither," he added.

At first I didn't know what he was talking about, but then I understood that he had been locked up for his shenanigans and was home for the brief holiday break. I smiled back at Marcus as I placed the canned goods on the shelf and said, "It's good to see you Marcus."

When I was Marcus' and Walter's age, my toughest chore was being forced to study Hebrew for my bar mitzvah. I got three meals a day, accompanied by all the chocolate cupcakes I could eat. I can only fantasize that if I were President, I would give every kid in the nation, legal, illegal, or natural-born citizen, the right to a free trip to Disneyland.

Walter didn't get to buy his Disney shirt at the park; he got it through a chance donation at a shelter. But Walter was going to make it. Even though his dealt hand was dismal, he was a righteous boy, a blessed kid. He was more grown up and had more guts than most adults I knew.

Seeing his Disney shirt made this place a small world after all. I reached in my pocket and handed him ten bucks. The funny thing was that Walter didn't have any hair, not a blade for the barber to cut and, frankly, I didn't care.

Walter lifting. *Photo by Steve Weintraub.*

23

Bien Sabrosa: The Taco Party

"Ya know, he's got six fingers, Marshall!" Reggie shared with me while leaning in extra close. Reggie's 8-year-old neighbor tagging along with him had an extra set of pinkies.

I told Reggie, then 12 years old, that I had noticed, and it wasn't important to go around telling people about his unusual find. Reggie was the kind of kid who, instead of walking around a puddle, would step directly into it, deeply in fact, in order to appreciate its essence. If you have ever been a camp counselor and taken kids on a walk-about, you'll know there is always one kid walking too close to the trail-edge separating him from a sheer drop, exercising his God-given right to gravity.

Reggie's tall, thin body reminded me of a new asparagus stalk announcing itself in the early spring, or as he himself proudly put it, "Man, I'm a bunch of bony body parts!"

To promote responsibility among kids at the gym, we developed "gym dollars." Every time someone helped with a task, showed a good report card, or completed a workout, that kid would earn a gym dollar that could be used for outings to the movies, amusement parks, or skating rinks.

For over two weeks, on a daily basis, Reggie had approached me like an investigative reporter to calculate his odds of attending the next event. On this day he said, "I got 19 gym dollars. How much does it cost to go skatin'?" I stared at his afro, which hadn't seen a pick in days, and told him it would cost 12 gym dollars. He, in turn, stared at me for a long moment, as though calculating the difference between the speed of sound and the speed of light. You could see the gears turning subtracting 12 gym dollars from 19. "I got me enough gym dollars to go skatin!" he shouted out proudly.

I found Reggie's spirit inspirational. He put up with a lot of teasing from the other kids. They called him, "Bony Ass." Sometimes he would cry over it. Still, he got back in the saddle to ride in life's rodeo again. Reggie had the priceless gifts of courage and inner-strength.

Sixty-pound Reggie loved coming to the gym, working out, and playing games. He often appeared in a bright-red, polo-type shirt with a wilted collar. Stitched on the left chest of that shirt was the emblem for the Schnucks market chain. A bagger's shirt, it must have been donated to Goodwill. Unlike Reggie, when I was a kid I had all kind of shirts. I remember frowning when I opened a birthday present to find a shirt instead of a toy. And yet here was Reggie, limited to one Count Chocula promotional T-shirt and a single polo shirt from the nearest Goodwill store. But to Reggie, something was better than nothing.

Reggie was one of the kids that I ferried home every evening in my rundown '85 Camaro. I love my car! The rear passenger compartment is slanted like a green, downhill ski run. You can feel the wheels pulling toward the equator whenever you make a left turn.

Occasionally, for a treat, I would take the kids to Del Taco to pick up a few six-packs of hard tacos for the ride home. Life hasn't been experienced fully until you've had a hard-shell taco party in an old, hoopty car. It's an open-mic, jazz jam session of crunching, chomping, and lip smacking.

Weeks later I could find remnants of beef in the car's faded-black interior. Invariably, a friend will end up pointing out that I have a piece of finely-shredded cheddar cheese stuck to the seat of my wrinkle-proof Dockers.

Reggie wore his Count Chocula T-shirt to one of these taco parties. It was one of his favorite shirts. To us it was one of those promotional shirts that you get when you send in two box tops and the chump change for shipping and handling. But to Reggie, the shirt looked half cool, especially since it was October. As he hurriedly ate several of the tacos that he drenched in fire-roasted hot sauce, dribbles of sauce would land haphazardly on the Count's fangs.

I dropped the kids off at their apartments one at a time. Reggie, however, took off so quickly he left Deonyia behind.

Deonyia lived with Reggie. If you're a teacher, Deonyia's the kind of kid you want in your classroom. She'll tell you if someone is copying homework or cheating. She takes it upon herself to straighten kids up, by saying, "Just plain act'n a fool."

I was impressed with Deonyia's skills at detecting misbehavior because she squinted all day. I couldn't see how she functioned at school.

Deonyia lived with her grandmother, mother, two sisters, a brother, several cousins, a small collection of cats, and a few displaced uncles who would conveniently come for "power stays" at the end of each month.

Deonyia needed a simple pair of eyeglasses. Her overwhelmed grandmother could barely keep up with the family let alone take the time to get Deonyia fitted for glasses. So we stepped in to help. Lawanda, one of the employees at the gym, was designated to take Deonyia and her mother for the appointment. Now she could function in school and in life.

As Deonyia opened the door to get out of the Camaro, she said softly, "Marshall, I'll give you this taco that I can't eat if you be my friend."

I smiled as I panned her run-down building with the sheets of cardboard covering several missing window panes, only to think: love and friendship isn't for sale in this Camaro. I replied, "whether you give me that hard-shell taco or not, I'm your friend."

"Marshall, I'll see you at the gym on Friday!" she called.

As the door slammed, the Camaro's hanging black interior, barely held up by several strategically placed safety pins, brushed against my forehead, like a curtain closing on a good play. I drove away, burping softly from a good meal, with the thought that these nine kids wouldn't go to bed hungry on this one night.

24

La Masquerade

Sometimes I feel like I've seen or heard it all. Other times I'm reminded of just how little I know.

Take Victoria Abernathy. She started coming to the gym simply because she lived across the alley from Mr. Lewis, our gym driver.

She was enthusiastic and was always pushing herself. Soon I began taking her to competitions along with the other kids. She slowly started blossoming into a competitive athlete. Although playful, she was eager to better herself at each meet, always seeking to lift more weight. Victoria would eventually become the player to beat at local competitions.

Victoria was part of our small entourage at the Junior Olympics in New Orleans. She won the gold medal, a great accomplishment for a 12-year-old from an impoverished neighborhood. When her name was announced she pranced to the victory in utter joy. I teared up as I watched her smile brightly at the top of the podium. What a well-earned boost to her self-esteem!

A year later, she qualified for the Junior Nationals in Flagstaff, Arizona. The best teenagers in the country compete there. I thought this would be a good steppingstone for Victoria. In fact, it was a huge accomplishment for any teenager to even qualify.

Victoria trained with her teammates four times a week for months. She enjoyed working out. You could see her intensity and sense of accomplishment. But one day out of nowhere, she stopped coming to the gym.

At first I thought nothing of it and figured it was probably due to cold-and-flu season until Treasure, her best friend, came to me prior to a workout. "Hey, did you hear what happened to Victoria?" she whispered, as if inviting me into a web of intrigue.

"She was almost raped."

I quickly asked if Victoria was all right. "I think she's in the hospital,"

Treasure responded.

Later that night, I tried to reach Victoria's mother, but since she didn't have a telephone, tracking her down wasn't easy. I called the two childrens hospitals in St. Louis and was swiftly shut down because I wasn't a relative. So I pulled an end run and asked Mr. Lewis to go on the hunt and find out why she had stopped coming to the gym.

He learned from neighbors that Victoria's family had moved across the river to East St. Louis. With some further digging, he located the address and telephone number.

I called her mother to find out what had happened. It turned out that a stranger in a car had tried to coax her inside, but Victoria knew better and ran off. Her mother said they moved in with her family across the river simply because she needed to move.

It's amazing how the rumor mill puts a spin on a story, but I was relieved that nothing worse had happened. The question now was how to get Victoria back to the gym. Though it added time onto his van schedule, Mr. Lewis understood that it was important for Victoria to continue. When she returned to the gym and was able to see her friends, she was overflowing with excitement.

Eventually Victoria moved back across the river. Since Mr. Lewis and I divided the kids to take home, I dropped off Victoria and the other kids who lived near me. Victoria always insisted on being dropped off last. I just figured she wanted to socialize longer with the other kids. Since she lived close to my house it didn't matter.

There was a Checkers Restaurant across the street from her drop off point. Occasionally I'd give her a buck to buy the 89-cent cheeseburger that was promoted in huge letters on the front window. When she didn't go to the Checkers for a quick fix of cooked ground beef and melted cheese, I would watch her walk into the seven-story apartment building to make sure she got in safely. She'd walk into the tiny vestibule, pick up the phone, and dial her mom to get "buzzed in."

One evening, I decided to switch the route going home just to break up the monotony. When I told Victoria that I would drop her off first, she didn't like it one bit. She tried to argue the point with me. When that didn't work, she moodily said that she wanted to be dropped off at the day care center a block up from her apartment building.

I pulled into the empty parking lot where she directed me and watched her walk behind the building. After she got out of the car, I realized that there was no day care sign anywhere in sight. Lavaughn, another gym kid, was in the car with me. I looked at his peanut shaved silhouette in the light from the Flaco Taco's neon sign, and we both said simultaneously, like a barbershop duet, "I hope she made it in." We looked at each other. Without saying a word, I pulled behind the building. Seeing nothing, we assumed she had gone inside.

A few days later I drove to the front of her apartment building, but instead of walking in through the front as usual, she cut through the unlit grass lawn to the rear of the building. Watching her walk down the dark alley, I pulled around to the other side and told Lavaughn, another gym kid, to ask her where she was going. "The front door is closed. I'm goin through the back," she replied over her shoulder with an attitude of "Whateverrr!" We drove off thinking nothing of it.

A month later, after one of the local weightlifting competitions, I got a call from Victoria's mom asking me where her daughter was. Exhausted from taking 28 kids to an all-day event, I listened as her mother, who was at work, asked me to find her, because she wasn't at home, and to take her home immediately, if not sooner. I felt responsible, thinking that perhaps she had gone to a friend's house after the competition.

My only wish on my one day off, with just three hours left before bedtime, was to watch a movie. I reluctantly reassured Victoria's mother that I would find her daughter and bring her home.

I cursed as I slowly re-stepped into the jeans I had worn for the past twelve hours. I hopped into the cold gym van with Carla at my side who wanted to spend time with me, and headed toward north St. Louis. Through a hunch and a prayer, we happened to spot Victoria walking. We pulled up beside her and told her we were taking her home.

I gave her a short speech about responsibility, while simultaneously thinking how badly I wanted to see *Schindler's List* on television. The responsibility speech sounded much like Charlie Brown's nagging teacher… Even I wasn't listening to it.

At the front of her apartment building, we waited until she got out. It's startling how puzzles appear easy at the end, when there are only a few mismatched pieces left. Amazing also how God can work.

As before, Victoria darted across the front lawn and around the side to the rear of the apartment building. Carla suggested, "Let's go make sure she gets in." Concurring, I pulled the van to the rear as we watched her ascend the fire escape. There was only enough light from the adjoining street lights to see her silhouette. We watched as she walked up five flights in the dark and she waved us off. Then Carla asked in a peculiar tone, "What kind of entrance is that?" But I was used to seeing the living conditions of some of the kids and didn't think anything of it.

Again, as she stood on the fifth-floor platform of the fire escape, Victoria attempted to wave us off. I tried to rationalize this by telling Carla that the front door was more than likely locked.

"This isn't right!" Carla said and rolled down the car window.

She called for Victoria to come down. Victoria dashed down the metal stairs, opened the door, and climbed back in the van.

"Go up here," she said forlornly and pointed up the alley.

I rolled to the next block, coasting like a hang glider before she said, "Stop here."

Silence enveloped the van as I read the red sign on the exterior of the building —"Salvation Army's Family Haven." I glanced at Carla as she turned around to see Victoria. I don't recall which one of us mouthed the standard, "It's okay, everything will be all right," but this attempt to encourage and show hope didn't stem the tears that streamed down Victoria's cheeks.

She stepped out of the vehicle and said, "See you tomorrow," and with that slammed the door shut. We watched as she walked through the homeless shelter's front door.

"I'm so dumb," I told Carla. "All this time I thought she lived in that apartment building. She sure fooled me."

Carla replied: "She's probably really embarrassed to live in a homeless shelter."

"No wonder she always wanted to be dropped off last," I said. "It's so simple if you put the puzzle together."

"Yeah," said Carla, "that's why the Salvation Army comes up on caller ID when she calls the house."

On the drive home, I puzzled about why we weren't doing more to help the homeless and displaced, especially our children.

I didn't see Victoria for a couple of days after that. By then it was time to go to the weightlifting competition in Arizona.

As I honked the horn on Lindell Boulevard outside the Salvation Army's Family Haven, I wondered about the stress on a person living there, especially a teenager.

Victoria wasn't downstairs in the lobby as planned, so I called the receptionist from my car phone and asked where she was. Meanwhile, curiosity was simmering in my brain like a pot of overcooked soup. I had a million questions that I wanted answered.

The receptionist told me, "She'll be right down." As I clicked the "end call" button on my cell phone, I knew that anyone with a half-functioning cerebellum who dealt with teenage girls knew it would be another fifteen minutes…at least. I stepped out of my Camaro and headed for the entry.

I pressed the doorbell and waited to get buzzed in. While at the entrance, I noticed the empty plant beds along the entrance and thought, "Hey I should get the local Gateway Gardening Club to donate some flowers and spruce up this institutionalized lobby." But that thought faded quickly as I pulled the door open. Stepping inside the hallway to a medium security-type setting, I looked around and wondered which way to go. The staff looked at me wondering if I was a social worker or juvenile officer checking up on an active case.

I noticed a chalkboard with the surnames of families in residence. Everything in this place seemed temporary and transitional, a name is wiped off with an eraser, readying the board for the next family.

While climbing the stairs, I peered out the window and observed that my car was parked half-cocked and blocking part of the driveway, as though for an ill-fated bank heist needing a quick get-away. At the top of the second floor, I stood looking at another locked door with a small intercom.

A staff person came out of the locked door, and I quickly grabbed it and walked in. I saw a case worker behind a small, clear glass window of the kind you see at a doctor's office. She somehow knew who I was and smiled as if we had known each other for the past ten years.

"Victoria didn't come down yet?" she asked placidly.

"No not yet."

So the caseworker put the stainless steel microphone to her lips, as though about to sing a jazz solo, but instead announced, "Victoria Abernathy, please come to the receptionist!" Her voice bounced through the cinder block hallway.

She told me to have a seat in the TV room to the right, and said she'd send someone to find her. I was in one of those perpetually tired states and welcomed the chance to sit down. After a few minutes of sitting, I stood up and began to pace the room like a large animal in a small cage. A staff person walked by and said, "She'll be down in a second."

A child playing near the window called me over, pointed to the double glass window, and explained as proudly as if he'd discovered penicillin, "Ya see if it was a bullet, it would have went through both." Then, like a TV detective, he scratched the BB pellet hole on the outside of the window with his tiny finger.

"You must be Victoria's coach?" he asked as if already knowing the answer. I smiled and answered affirmatively.

"You lift weights? She strong? What days the gym open?"

He shot question after question leaving no time for a response. His questions brought another smile to my face. You could tell by his body language and questions that he was a confident and smart boy.

I could only think to myself, shame on us for what these kids have to go through in life. When I was his age, I was shooting off fireworks, building play forts, and riding my bike to the local Dairy Queen. But these kids were spending their wonder years in a homeless shelter.

"Can you come take us to the gym?" he asked.

"Talk to Victoria when we get back, and we'll see what we can do," I replied.

I walked back over to the caseworker and began gently interrogating her. "How many rooms do you have here?"

"We have two floors this side, and on the west side the rooms are about the size of this room, about 8 feet by 10 feet. Some families have to share a room."

"You mean they sleep in a room with strangers? I was surprised at that. "So do Victoria and her mother share a room with others?"

"Yes, they share a room with another three or four people."

Now depressed, I said, "Oh."

"It's better than nothin'," she shot back.

"Here she is," chimed in another staff member, pointing to Victoria. Victoria had a smile on her face as she walked proudly down the hall towards me with her freshly gelled hair and a quart bottle of activator in her hands.

I guess I felt I was rescuing her for this brief out-of-town weightlifting competition. But the fact was that after this trip to Arizona, she was coming back to this temporary shelter, whereas I would be returning to a spacious house in a better neighborhood. What I find most disturbing is that there are thousands of kids out there just like Victoria, who need a drop here, or a sprinkle there, just to make it in times of trouble, in times of need.

Eventually, we left the shelter and went to pick up Victoria's friend Lateisha so they could spend the night at our house and catch a plane to Phoenix early in the morning. On the way to Lateisha's, I asked Victoria if she was all right. She said she was. I pushed a little more, trying to get her to talk about why she had created a "cover-up operation" and hadn't been forthcoming about living in the shelter.

She responded, "It's embarrassing staying in a shelter; none of my friends are around."

I replied, "If you ever want to talk about it, let me know. I can't imagine how hard it is for you."

"Okay, but my Momma is fixin on moving out of that place soon," she said confidently. She then reached for the buttons on the radio and turned the music up a notch. That signaled the end of the conversation. I knew that although she didn't want to talk about it then, she knew she could count on Carla and me if she ever did need to talk.

Victoria had a great time on the trip, with Laesha along for companionship. She did well at the Junior Nationals, took her first plane ride and hiked the Grand Canyon.

Victoria works full-time, has two kids and an apartment.

Victoria (right) and Laesha at the Grand Canyon after representing Lift For Life Gym at the Junior Nationals in Arizona.

25

Genuine

In our travels through life, we are given the grand opportunity to encounter many people, some with questionable lifestyles, some just ordinary folk. But rarely are we blessed to meet and be friends with a young man like Terry Moore. I had the good fortune to be a father figure to this wonderful person. It wasn't so much what I, as a role model, gave to Terry, but what we learned from each other that made our relationship genuine and special.

In 1990, this toothpick-sized kid came strolling into the gym on Washington Avenue, trailing behind his older brother Raymond. He had come along to lift weights because Raymond couldn't leave him home alone and didn't want to miss the gym. I didn't think much of it, a young, skinny kid who could barely curl a five-pound dumbbell, let alone get it off the rack.

For the first couple of months, I didn't pay much attention to him until one day, while Raymond and the other kids took off down the street to Union Station for fun, games, and a little trouble, Terry stayed behind to help me clean up. Since they had just moved to a new apartment, Raymond assured me from halfway down the block that Terry knew where he lived. I asked Terry, and he also reassured me that he did.

That was until 30 minutes later, when he climbed into my car, got comfortable in the rear seat, snapped the seatbelt shut, and somehow magically forgot. So for the next hour, Terry, Carla, and I drove around the city looking for his new apartment amid the vast inventory of low-income housing developments in the city. After we had gone to every neighborhood in midtown, downtown, this town and that town, searching for something that would remotely jog his memory, he finally recognized his apartment. It was an hour ride that should have taken about four minutes.

So this slight inconvenience opened a new, refreshing chapter in my life. The ride had given us time to connect. I learned who Terry was, what school he attended, and what TV shows he watched.

As Terry came to the gym, little by little, the five-pound weights turned into 10-pounders, the 10-pounders into 15. And not only did he come every day the gym was open, he started stepping up and doing little odd jobs around the gym, like cutting and serving the birthday cake, making sure he cooked the barbecue and not me, because, as he said while dramatically swinging the tongs in my face, "You don't know how to cook barbecue, Marshall. I'll do it!"

While some of the other kids would go off and steal cars, or hang out in rough areas and participate in questionable activities, Terry had a plan — to get a job, finish high school, go off to college, and live an honorable and humble life.

Soon Terry started helping me at Globe Drug. The other employees were used to the gym kids I had allowed to work in the store: playful, a little unconventional, etc., but Terry had seriousness and determination, gifts that earned him higher-end duties, like running the cash register, the filet mignon job at the store. Terry gained respect for his honesty and even

Terry (left), twin brother Gary and Michael help me barbecue after a workout on Washington Avenue. *Photo by Carla Scissors-Cohen.*

won over my two skeptical aunts, Rose and Sylvia. Had we been a more sophisticated retail operation, Terry would have monopolized the employee-of-the-month award.

A quiet kid, Terry knew that by lying back like a hunter and waiting for the prey to emerge, he would succeed. This skill became vital in cutting our shoplifting. He was able to catch employees and customers alike for thievery.

So while I was focused on selling goods and a little in my own world, Terry often interrupted me while I was negotiating a big sale to say, "Marshall, that guy just shoved a pack of socks down the front of his pants," or, "There's a man in the bathroom eat'n a can of your Vienna sausages and crackers." After a time, I learned from him not to be so focused on working with wholesale customers and making fancy Saks Fifth Avenue displays throughout our dingy discount store that I failed to pay attention to the thievery that abounded. It wasn't so much me teaching Terry, but Terry teaching me.

But the most compelling life lesson I learned from Terry, something that humbles me to this day, was to pay attention to *all* the kids, not just the strongest. In the early years of the gym, my focus had been on winning medals and trophies. As I matured, I learned that everyone is a winner, regardless of size and the two-bit medals they were able to hang around their necks.

Terry frequently came to our home and pleasantly maneuvered himself into our lives. Like a matched set of tablecloth and napkins, we clicked as a family. We discussed life, compared and contrasted Judaism and Christianity, talked about money and how to make it in the world. Terry chastised me for failing to understand the subtleties of barbecuing, while Carla and I provide an initiation to the joys of matzo ball soup and gefilte fish during Passover. He frequented our lives so much that one spring afternoon as Carla and Terry were driving to Blockbuster to get a movie, they were the lucky recipients of some racial profiling.

They were pulled over by the guys in blue, who questioned if Carla was "all right." They had figured that something was amiss with a black teenager driving a car with a white woman as a passenger. That didn't sit well with her, and she tongue-lashed the officer for several minutes.

As he continued to come to the gym and took on more responsibilities, his interest in helping kids blossomed. An opportunity for advancement in our little gym usually meant cutting the occasional birthday cake or coaching younger kids spiked with Attention Deficit Disorder. But then one day we received a generous grant from the United Way for a small storefront satellite gym in the Forest Park Southeast Neighborhood. Terry was the perfect candidate to manage that project.

Terry's caring and nurturing skills were exceptional. He had antennas, or should I say the ability, to spot a bad home life. He made it a point to include all kids, especially the ones he could tell were struggling with life's harsh challenges. There was one group of boys in particular who were struggling because of their home life. Terry adopted them without all the paperwork and made sure they stayed straight. He took them swimming, to the movies, played kickball with them, and became a wonderful role model. Keep in mind that Terry himself came from a single-parent, low-income family. He was a twin and the last out of the womb, the baby of the family.

For his first ten years, Terry's family lived in the projects, the awful kind that stacks a bunch of desolate people into a twelve-floor tower and then multiplies it by six more towers a pebble's throw away. He occasionally discussed with me the goings-on at the projects and became frustrated when I looked startled from his tales of daily shootings, kids joyriding on top of the elevators, and the abundance of drugs being sold. It sounded to me like a Wild-West show 24/7. For Terry to make it out of there was an absolute act of God. Years from now, I think, people will look back on projects like those and wonder what the social planners could have been thinking when they built such counterintuitive monstrosities. Did they actually think cramming a bunch of people in a small space would breed success?

Terry was determined to get a car. He asked us to teach him to drive at every waking moment. He passed the driver's test after two or three attempts and was able to purchase a car with his earnings. That impressed his peers. Someone they knew could actually get a car the honest way and not have to jack it from a lot using a flathead screwdriver as a key.

Given his point of origin, Terry's getting to college was like someone trekking up Mount Kilimanjaro with a peanut butter sandwich and a leaky bottle of water. He made it to graduation day by running the satellite gym in the evenings and working at J.C. Penney.

Eventually, Terry moved north to Minnesota to get a degree in broadcasting. After receiving his degree and returning to St. Louis, he continued working.

Then one day I got a call from Terry's older brother Raymond, the first kid to come to the gym. "Did you hear about Terry?" he asked in a distressed voice. "We'd been trying to reach you — he only has days left to live!"

My knees buckled when I heard this. I figured Terry would be visiting ME in a nursing home when I got old. This is not how it is supposed to be.

I darted to the hospital and made it to the intensive care unit. Terry was in a small glass room. Because of his advanced-stage disease, he couldn't be around any germs. Outside the room, I dressed in disposable hospital blues, the same kind I wore when my daughters were born. I found Terry grasping for every free breath that we take for granted. Cables, tubes, wires, everything running this way and that out of his body. God…why him?

Being challenged with sickle cell anemia had never stopped Terry. For as far back as I can remember, Terry would go in and out of the hospital when it flared up—most of his young life. But while many would use illness as an excuse, Terry wouldn't have it. He was stubborn and would never surrender, no retreat. No disease was going to stop him from reaching where he had to go. But this time would be different.

As I walked in, he barely raised his arm to motion a lifeless welcome. I sat down in the only chair in the room, shocked at the level of deterioration to the well-groomed and fit Terry that I once knew. I held his hand tightly and told him that I loved him, that he was one of my favorite kids, that he was like a son to me, all the while spewing a fire hydrant's supply of tears.

As always, Terry remained calm, strong, and determined. Moments later one of his church members burst into the room and reached out her hands as though smack in the middle of a well-written Sunday sermon. In an animated voice, she asked Terry, "Well…what do you want to do?"

"Fight!" Terry replied in his high-pitched voice. That summed up who Terry was, along with determination, perseverance, consistency.

This city is a better place because of Terry. There might not be a street named after him, or a monument, but he is a cornerstone in the lives of so many kids that he helped.

May his memory be a blessing.

Terry and I pose for a publicity shot outside the gym.
Photo by Steve Weintraub.

26

Innocent Giant

Some kids stand out because of their personalities; others because of their physicality. Cornelius Harris caught my attention at first because he was so big. At age 11, he was already five feet, 10 inches tall. He was strong and, because of his fascination with weights, was getting stronger.

For a couple of years we had a wrestling program. Boris Khodsov, our volunteer wrestling coach was from the former Soviet Union. His athletes had included two medalists from the Barcelona Olympics. Boris would regularly rhapsodize in his thick Russian accent that big kids like Cornelius "are unbelievable! In Russia, we would go around to different cities to find these kids." His voice would drop conspiratorially as he leaned in to confide as if telling me a classified state secret: "Marshall, very few. Very few," he would repeat. "In a town, maybe one in four or five thousand kids are like this kid."

Cornelius (third from left) with his first place trophy at the Junior Nationals, Albuquerque, NM.

Cornelius came to the gym religiously with the cousins who brought him. He loved to lift but also to play with his friends. You could tell he was starved for social opportunities. I imagined him cooped up like a caged bird in his house, not allowed to go outside and play in the hood. He came alive at the gym.

When Cornelius arrived, he would go right to the weights and work out relentlessly. Then he shot an hour of hoops, played games, and listened to rap music on our dysfunctional radio that worked every so often or when someone held the antenna doing a yoga triangle pose.

But on one particular day, just after we got started lifting weights, a large woman entered the gym and stood impatiently at the door. Angry and agitated, the steam seemed to flow out of her ears.

"Neal," she bellowed, as she peered around the gym. "You get your ass out here!"

As I approached the door, I turned in time to see Cornelius wipe a layer of thick sweat off his forehead and place the dumbbells back in the rack. Embarrassed, he dragged himself slowly toward his mother.

"Come on, get over here!" she barked. "You ain't hangin around here!"

His mom yanked Cornelius by the arm. "My son ain't workin out at no homosexual gym!" she yelled at me. "He ain't never comin back!"

She made her point as she dragged her son out the door without giving me any chance to tell her about the program. I could only focus on Cornelius' face full of tears.

I thought to myself, "I'm only trying to help. Dang lady, I'm not a pedophile, give me a break. I don't even get paid."

"Don't worry, Marshall," one of the teenagers reassured me. "She's goin through some rough times."

After some months, I learned that Cornelius was living in a halfway house with his mother and two brothers, a place for addicts trying to break away from crack cocaine. I pondered going there to attempt a normal conversation with the mother, to explain to her what the gym was all about, but I didn't want a repeat of her previous performance.

Two months later while I was at work, putting discount gallons of bleach on the shelves, I heard a soft voice echo through the canyon of cleaning products: "Marshall, ya think I can start com'n back to the gym?"

I turned to find Cornelius under the flickering florescent lights. Our innocent giant had returned.

"My mama said I can start com'n back to the gym," he said.

Over the years Cornelius turned into a dominator. Every contest, every competition he entered, he would win. We traveled all over the country: Florida, Iowa, and New Mexico, to name only a few. He even won the title in his weight class at the Junior Nationals sponsored by the United States Weightlifting Association.

Cornelius' world opened up when he took his first plane ride on a trip to New Mexico for the Junior Nationals. We visited the Native American cliff dwellings, ate at authentic Mexican restaurants that made the fast food chains look like an insult to humanity, and, best of all, took him and another athlete skiing after the competition. Cornelius didn't care how many times he fell in the snow. After a while, thanks to the private ski instructor we hired for an hour, he figured it out and had a blast. When we returned to St. Louis, he was never the same. Driven was an understatement; Cornelius was going to make it in life and make it big.

Most importantly, Cornelius stayed in school, and that was the whole point of the program. Sure it's great to be the best as an athlete, but school isn't a second tier choice.

At Lift For Life's five year anniversary party, the Mayor of St. Louis, Freeman Bosley, was handing out awards to successful gym members, including, of course, Cornelius. As I scanned the audience of parents and reporters, my eyes fell on Cornelius's mom. I was gratified to see how proud she was of Cornelius' award. "That's my boy!" her smile indicated, like a bright headlight shining on a dark, backcountry Alabama road.

At the end of the ceremony, she approached me, the same woman who years earlier had exploded through the gym in a fit of rage. "Marshall, remember when I made that comment to you years ago?" she asked.

I shook my head silently.

"Well," she continued after a slight pause, "I want to say I am sorry for what I said. I was going through some rough times, but that's all behind me. You're doing a wonderful thing down here with these kids — you should be proud of yourself. The Lord is gonna bless you!"

What nice words to hear on our five year anniversary.

Cornelius graduated from high school. I'll cherish the memory of his ceremony forever. When Cornelius' name was announced, the entire auditorium burst into applause, not just because he was popular, but because he was one of a handful of graduates to receive a scholarship to college. The scholarship was to a community college, and, best of all, it was in sunny Arizona; the state next to New Mexico where we had enjoyed our momentous trip years before. Cornelius would be the first in his family to attend college.

I had initially seen Cornelius as a tree, young and frail, blowing back and forth in the wind. That tree had grown tall and thick through the years and was now strong enough to withstand a gale.

The definition of making it big, in my opinion, is not becoming rich and famous, but picking yourself up from the pit, regardless of what has happened to you, making a full recovery and transforming yourself to becoming a lifetime winner.

I received a picture and letter from Cornelius while he was in college in Arizona. The card read, "Just when I reached the end of my rope…you were there for me. Thanks." He added a very special note in his own words: "You have always been there in times of need; never showing a needy kid one ounce of greed. Think of all the kindness you've shown. It's the reason why I have matured and grown."

Cornelius currently resides in Scottsdale, Ariz., with his wife and two children. His younger brothers, John and Aaron, attended the charter school we started, and Aaron recently graduated from high school.

Neil's mother started counseling addicts and has helped many people recover.

Cornelius tries skiing after winning first place at the Junior Nationals in New Mexico.

27

The Verbal Eviction

The revitalization of Washington Avenue had reached a tipping point. Little by little, legitimate businesses were replacing the alternative commerce of drugs, prostitution, and unlicensed businesses. Our new landlords, Bob Scullin and his wife, were downright nice folk who bent over backwards to help our mission.

Still, Bob needed to make changes to create cash flow. The crazy Swiss-chalet design of the building and the lack of funds to fully rehab and resuscitate it created challenges. Having a gym anchor one corner of the building and inner-city kids congregating outside on the sidewalk, made it difficult to lure tenants.

The day came in 1997. Bob requested apologetically that the gym move out. He asked how much time we needed. At first I was offended. His *fashtunkina* (Yiddish for *funky*) building was 80 percent empty. "How dare he ask us to leave!"

It took me a few years to get over moving out of that building. And to this day, I regret my actions. I notified the *St. Louis Post-Dispatch* and expressed my indignation over our situation. Out of anger, I said some things in the paper that weren't nice. Bob and his wife were fair, and business was business. As the Godfather Michael Corleone always said, "It's not personal."

Although moving was difficult, sometimes the path ahead is better. I just didn't know it at the time.

We scrambled to move into our satellite gym while we regrouped and figured out our game plan. The satellite was in a small brick building situated off Cherokee Street, a main drag in south St. Louis. Back in the '50s and '60s, Cherokee Street functioned as a small town main street. With one retail establishment after another, it was the place to shop for all your needs. Then it fell into decline. People who used to live in the area blamed it on "them coloreds moving in."

Our satellite was a 20-step dance from the business strip. It measured 1,500 square feet and couldn't hold more than 20 kids, let alone workout equipment and a couple of coaches. If more kids showed up, they spilled out onto the sidewalk, hung out and enjoyed themselves. Area business owners felt "these" kids were hurting their bottom lines. The writing on the wall was clear.

One thing that's for sure in this world: if you don't go for it, it ain't com'n to ya. The heat continued from the business owners. So I decided to roll the dice and take out a small ad in the *Ladue News* asking for "help" to buy a building.

Ladue News is one of those "stylish" magazines that highlights all the ins and outs of the wealthy in the community, a "society paper." It's the kind of publication that features people at black tie events and high-end businesses that sell *chochkas* (Yiddish for *knick-knacks*) and what-nots if you have a few extra discretionary dollars.

I figured, what the heck, we are down to one small gym that couldn't hold a handful of sardines. What's three hundred bucks for an ad if it helps us secure a permanent home.

Business professors would tell you that marketing is cumulative. You need to run several ads and use other avenues, like direct mail, to reach your audience. Yet as unplanned luck would have it, a week or two after the magazine came out, we received a call.

Steve Tschudy said that he and his family wanted to "learn more about the gym". It's a phrase I'd heard before. Most of the time, these calls don't pan out. But Steve sounded sincere, and I had nothing to lose, so I sent him some information about our program.

Around the same time, a friend from temple suggested I call Eric Friedman, a local real estate broker. Here we were, no money whatsoever. And yet, here's a guy that cared enough about about kids to take time out of his busy schedule to parade me around town to look at properties.

Eric and I finally found a low income area, saturated with vacant lots and abandoned warehouses and sprinkled with a few struggling business. The building that caught our attention was an old truck repair garage that measured 5,000 square feet. Soon after, we set up an appointment to explore this great find.

As Eric and I walked in, we realized why the broker needed the owner to show the property. Either he was frightened of the few small mammals scurrying about, or he needed help turning on the lights. Or both. The electrical set-up was unique and probably not up to code. In an attempt to properly show us the property, the owner plugged in an extension cord to power a couple of fluorescent lights hanging above. Still too dark, he opened the garage door at the end of the building so we could see.

What was revealed mimicked the set of "*Sanford and Sons*" without all the *shmatas* (Yiddish for *trash*). I remember the broker checking our faces for a "what the fuck is this place?" reaction. But Eric and I were totally used to *fashtunkina* properties and weren't fazed one bit. Price was our driving point; the more a place needed repairs, the better the price for us.

The building was located on Cass Avenue just north of downtown in a neighborhood known as Old North St. Louis. It was a single story, cinder block structure that featured a mural of Olympic boxer and St. Louisan Leon Spinks. It definitely had that special Lift For Life flava.

The building featured a large open space, warped plywood sheets covering the windows, small rodents scurrying about, and of course, a single toilet in the rear of the building without walls. It did have a few green, dingy drop cloths protecting the view if you needed to take a leak in private.

Best of all, the price tag was just $42,000 and was accompanied by two large parcels. The seller was hungry to make this deal happen. As a bonus, folks in this neighborhood wouldn't mind seeing our kids being kids.

The place needed to come alive—you could feel it. The building yearned for something more than grease stained floors and boarded up windows. We were just the group to give this building a facelift.

Eric worked his magic and negotiated attractive terms that included a second deed of trust with the current owner, Ralph Coldewe. This helped lower the amount needed for a down payment.

And as things fell into place, Steve, the guy who first called, sent word that his family would contribute a substantial gift to help purchase the building and support much of the renovation. The Tschudy's generosity made this location a "for sure thing" for Lift For Life. We'd never have to move again.

Now we could minimally fix up the place—redo the bathroom, install a furnace, change out a door or two. In Lift For Life language, minimally also means it was okay to have the plywood remain on the windows, and only add a couple more fluorescent fixtures.

In the early 1990s, when in line skating (aka Rollerblading) was popular, Carla and I put on races to raise money for the gym. We had hundreds of participants and made a little pocket change.

Most of the racers were teens or young adults attempting to roll through the streets of downtown as fast as possible without wiping out on a bumpy patch of asphalt. The fact that we were raising funds to help inner city kids wasn't on their radar screens.

Durb Curlee was different. Older than most of the other skaters, Durb cared about his race times, but he also seemed to care about the cause. Year after year he'd hang out after the race to chat about the competition, thank us for putting on the event, and ask a few questions about the gym. Usually I was too busy to talk.

One year, he said "My wife and I are interested in seeing what you are doing at the gym." Of course Carla chimed in, "That's great. We'd love to have you come down for a tour!"

The only thing going on in my thick skull was how little time I had left to tear down the race–pick up all the cones on the course, haul the tables and chairs back, pick up the trash, etc.

But then I figured, why not? I'll ask them down and show them our priceless wonder. Besides, this would end the conversation and I could get back to cleaning up.

Durb and his wife Ellen ventured down to Lift For Life shortly thereafter.

It's interesting what different people see when they look at the same picture.

We had a full house that afternoon. I was embarrassed about the funky light fixtures and the plywood still covering the windows. The sound of weights clanking bounced off the dingy walls. The rambunctious gym members were all getting on my nerves.

Durb and Ellen say they saw something different. They saw happy kids engaged in organized chaos. They saw a safe environment for kids with very few options. They saw an opportunity to help.

Durb asks, "So how much do you need to finish fixing up this place?" Caught off guard, I didn't have a clue how to respond. I'd never had anyone ask me that before. So I went into my peddler salesmanship routine of what we would like to get "redone." Durb attempted to extract an exact amount from me. He finally gave up and said, "We'll send you something."

When someone says something like that, you never know what to think. A $100 gift? $1,000 gift? Who knows? But when the check came in the mail, it was much larger than I ever dared to dream. We were finally able to install real windows, update the electric, fix the plumbing and have a working drinking fountain for our thirsty athletes. We no longer resembled the hole in the wall gym from the blockbuster *Rocky*.

There were countless other people and companies that joined our team–good-hearted folks and organizations that helped us establish solid footing in the community and guaranteed that we would be there for the kids for generations to come. Even Marshall Faulk, the Rams Football Hall of Famer, donated and helped raised money.

What's most profound is how many generous people stepped up to make sure that Lift For Life would always have a safe place for kids. Folks, too numerous to name here, who gave without asking for anything in return. No strings attached, no naming rights. Giving and flying under the radar, is the highest level of charity, *tzdeka*.

Hall of Fame football player Marshall Faulk with Lift For Life kids.

28

What Were You Doing When You Were Nine Years Old?

What *I* was doing was getting on my Mom's nerves, bugging her for money, so I could hop on my bike and ride a couple of uphill miles to the candy store to buy a 10-cent piece of "Bub's Daddy Bubble Gum," that gum with all the white, chalky powder on it. If you had a big enough mouth, you could jam in the entire log and still keep the saliva from drooling out. After chewing for twenty minutes, your jaw muscles would fail and your words would slur like a cassette player low on batteries.

Or I'd be watching countless repeats of *"Speed Racer"* and trying to read the lips of Christy or Speed and wondering why the words didn't match the movement of their mouths. Or pondering why Gilligan never made a pass at Mary Ann, or how living on that island for years with no grocery store, the anxious Skipper still kept putting on pounds.

What were you doing? Going to the movies? Shopping? Hanging out with friends? Eating ice cream?

As for me, not a worry in the world. My parents took care of me. Plenty of good food and a safe home. The only thing on my mind was whether my mom would yell at me for getting my pants so dirty. After a day of playing sports, I'd come home with so much grass and dirt on my pants they would have sprouted a lawn if you'd watered them with a hose. No problem, my mom had a stockpile of Tide.

So hyper-drive thirty years later: I'm surrounded by about 35 kids having a jump-rope contest. The winner will be whoever can jump the most revolutions per minute, but all the participants will get some kind of treat, whether gigantic jawbreakers that last a couple of decades, boxes of cereal, candy bars, paddle balls, or you name it. And guess what the most sought after prize is? The cereal.

One girl in particular has my attention. She weighs around 49 pounds, half the weight of my spotted Dalmatian. She jumps so quickly she reminds me of a dragonfly hovering over a murky pond on a windless, summer day. She looks like she is ready to go airborne in the gym. Others are less graceful, their pants drooping down to their ankles, needing to stop every two revolutions to pull up their britches, while the rest of the kids laugh hysterically.

I first noticed the new kid sitting as far back as the building would allow. Her face was pointing down at the blemished concrete floor. She appeared uncomfortable and overwhelmed around the energized group of regulars.

When it is her turn, she goes to the center of the wooden platform and picks up the rope. She wraps it around her tiny hands. Actually, it is a straight telephone cord, not a rope, because that is the choice of champions, inner-city kids. Telephone cords are quicker than regular jump ropes and in a kid's mind, they are free to take off the wall and borrow for a quick game of double-dutch. I ask the girl what her name is and write it down on the scorecard when she quietly replies, "Theresa."

I press the stopwatch and Theresa starts jumping, her fluffy ponytail bobbing up and down with every turn of the cord. Forty-five seconds into her turn, she abruptly stops and, without a word, walks back to her chair, picks up her half-eaten, three-piece Church's fried chicken box, and resumes eating her starchy biscuit. She has been looking down the entire time, as though trying not to step on any cracks in the floor for bad luck. The other kids turn to one another in silence, as if saying, "What's wrong with her?"

She had just stopped, as though the ideas of "completion" or "success" had been deleted from her repertoire. Or maybe it took more effort than she had to continue. Now we are all frozen in an eerie silence. To quickly change the somber climate, I shout out, "Next!" and activity recommences.

We wrap up the contest and pass out prizes to the eager group. Later we close the gym, and Mr. Lewis loads the van with kids to drive home. I notice Theresa sitting quietly on the bench, while her 8-year-old brother fights toothless aliens and steroid-enhanced monsters on a one of the free arcade games at the back of the building.

"Why aren't you getting on the van?" I ask.

Theresa says she is waiting for her mother.

How long before her mother comes? I ask. She shrugs her shoulders. Mr. Lewis motions for me to come over.

"It breaks my heart," says Mr. Lewis to me in a saddened voice.

"What? I don't understand," I respond.

"Ya know, they are livin' in the women's shelter down the street."

My head shakes in dismay. "Damn. Well, I'll wait with her for the mother to pick them up. You are shit if ya ain't got no money!"

"'You're right about that,'" he says, shaking his head in disappointment and turning to walk back to the gym van.

While we wait for Theresa's mother, I decide to catch up on my endless/infinite list of "to do's," so I ask her if she wants to help lay ceramic tiles in the bathroom we are renovating. I'm pleased when she eagerly agrees.

I grab a box of mismatched tiles in one arm, pick up the five-gallon bucket of mastic glue in the other, and proceed to the bathroom with light-skinned Theresa, who is dressed in a pink sparkled shirt with navy blue, platform tennis shoes, following behind. I spread the tile mastic on the floor like creamy peanut butter on a fresh piece of toast, and show Theresa where to place the tiles. Occasionally, she places the tiles a bit askew, but I know it is more beneficial for her to receive positive praise for her job than for me to adjust every single piece. Besides, it's a bathroom floor near the urinal.

As I spread the cement, Theresa pushes the tiles down into the cement, and we slowly begin to chat. I ask her my stock questions, like: How is the food at school? What's your favorite TV show? Your favorite subject, etc? She tells me her favorite subject is math. I ask her what she wants to be when she grows up. She replies, "a doctor," and strategically pushes a piece of the off-gray tile into the sticky cement.

I love to hear that answer from kids. Aim high! What an answer.

"So, how long have you been staying at that place?" I ask.

"Three days," she replies.

"How about before that?"

"We lived with our grandfather," she answers, softer than a mouse chewing cheese.

"It didn't work out?" I venture supportively.

She shakes her head quietly from side to side.

"What happened?"

"He came after my Momma with an ax."

"Oh," I say, feeling punched in the stomach. I hesitate. "That must have been pretty hard?"

"Yes," she says, as she hands me another tile from the box.

We continue to lay the flooring. The eerie silence again. What can an adult say to comfort a 9-year-old kid who should be playing with dolls and watching cartoons? "Oh, things will be better soon?" Is that going to help?

A half-hour passes. We start to clean up. Her mother returns for Theresa and her brother. The mother has to pry Theresa's brother off the video game; hopefully, he conquered the infestation of aliens.

I set the alarm and closed the door to the gym behind me, like closing another book, another memory of a kid, another reminder of why we need to help them. After driving home, I enter my house to be greeted warmly by my wife and licks from my two dogs. A nice home, a nice life. Yet I am saddened because I know that little Theresa is in a shelter with her eight-year-old brother. Someone else's place, someone else's bed, someone else's life.

"If ya don't get there by 9:00 p.m., they ain't goin' to let you stay; they put you out," she had explained to me earlier.

So, what were you doing when you were 9 years old?

29

THE TALE OF TWO CARS

What distinguished Lavaughn and his best friend, Keith, from the "average Joe" kids is they had the misfortune to grow up in a crime-ridden, 12-story high-rise project. Both were clean cut, good, honest, American kids.

Lavaughn, 9 years old, lived with his mother and older brother. His mother worked hard and was a very nice person who was interested in what her kids were doing, whether inside the house or out. The only problem was that she worked the evening shift. So while the boys were at school,

Lavaughn and Willie. *Photo by Carla Scissors-Cohen.*

she was at home; and when the boys were home from school, she was at work. This was a cocktail for any child's failure. Lavaughn's older brother had come to the gym, but eventually I'd kicked him out because he either brought trouble with him, or hung out with it in the projects.

Lavaughn was an excessively high-energy kid, who wanted to get involved with everything. He just wouldn't or couldn't sit for a long period of time in the classroom, say more than a few minutes out of an hour. He talked when he wasn't supposed to, interrupted his teachers, did whatever it took to make sure he was being noticed and entertaining.

Yet Lavaughn was extremely intelligent. You could tell, because even though his grades were pathetic, he argued like a lawyer. To say that Lavaughn tested my patience is an understatement. At times I wondered why I should continue letting him attend the gym, but I knew that I couldn't allow a 9-year-old energy-dosed kid dictate to me.

Keith was the complete opposite. Whereas Lavaughn expressed everything on his mind, Keith kept it to himself but studied everyone carefully, like a *National Geographic* photographer taking pictures of animals in a remote island in the Pacific.

When push came to shove, however, Keith knew how to voice his opinion. Like that one time when I took the kids out for dinner. Since my Camaro would only hold so many kids at once, I had to separate them for outings on different days. One night I took the kids who lived on the North Side to feast on tacos, and on the following night I took the kids who lived on the South Side, including Keith and Lavaughn, to get pizza. The next day, upset that he'd had to settle for pizza instead of crunchy tacos, Keith drew a fabulous picture of me, curly hair and all, accompanied by two black kids, one on my left and the other on my right, labeled Northside kids and Southside kids. Written underneath the drawing was: "Secondhand Southside Kids."

Keith lived with his grandmother because his mother, although a pleasant person, didn't have what it took to raise him successfully. To this day, he always refers to his grandmother as his mother. I have to hand it to all the grandmothers who take care of their grandbabies because their kids just can't get it together. I had countless kids at the gym whose only stabilizing factor at home was a together grandmother.

The crime-ridden projects where Lavaughn and Keith lived were located just across the viaduct from Globe, so it was natural that those two would become fixtures at the store and in my life. At first, they came to the store to hang out while waiting for me to take them to the gym with the other kids. But then they started coming even on days there was no gym, just because they enjoyed hanging out with me in a business environment, learning what it took to run a store, and watching the wide variety of customers.

Soon enough, Lavaughn and Keith worked their way into helping me with odd jobs and replaced the lint in their pockets with loose change. These two refused to waste their money on childish things. They would buy themselves shoes and other necessities when they could afford it. Sometimes, when there was no food in their cramped apartments, they would provide the meals.

I particularly remember Lavaughn and Keith telling me they had seen my homeless friend Eugene at St. Vincent's Church, which was known for providing free meals the last 10 days of the month. To them, going to a food shelter was just an ordinary part of their lives, and they just talked about it in casual conversation, the way other kids might debate which candy to buy with their allowance. Imagine that you and your friend walk without your parents down to the church for dinner because you don't have enough food to get you through the month.

One of their tasks on Saturday was going to Union Station to buy lunch. It was the highlight of the day: to leave work, go for a walk, and get paid to get lunch—it was the ultimate job for a kid. I never did the math, but I think that after I bought lunch for the three of us and paid them for going to pick it up, I could have paid for a gourmet dinner for two.

One day during our lunch feast, Lavaughn noticed I was playing the Monopoly game from McDonald's. You collect the game pieces to win prizes. Like the board game, the higher end "properties" win the bigger prizes. Park Place and Boardwalk would win you the ultimate prize for adults; a million dollars, before taxes of course. It seemed as though McDonald's had printed a zillion Park Place pieces, but only one Boardwalk. So, just like a drivers license, everyone in the continental United States that ate at McDonald's had the Park Place piece.

I never expected to win and gave some of the small, chump change prizes, like a free cheeseburger or a McMuffin sandwich, to the kids. Just for the fun of it, I held onto the Park Place piece.

Later in the week, when Lavaughn came to the store to hang out, he asked me if I could buy him something to eat, because he was hungry. I told him I would, and he dashed off to McDonalds. When he returned, while woofing down his lopsided Quarter Pounder with a few sliced pickles hanging overboard, he casually mentioned, "Oh, I have that piece," as he pointed with a half eaten fry sticking out the side of his mouth to the ultimate game piece, Boardwalk. See, Lavaughn was smart, he knew how to deliver information in such a way as to arouse maximum attention. He's kind of like the kid in summer camp who lets a green teenage counselor know there's a copperhead snake in the cabin wiggling around after everyone has finally calmed down from a pillow fight and snuggled fast asleep in their sleeping bags.

He mentioned it while I was on the phone. At first, I didn't think much of it, but halfway through a boring conversation with the other party about merchandise, I quickly said I had to go and asked Lavaughn to repeat himself.

"Yeah, I have that piece. It's at home on my dresser," he said nonchalantly while taking another large bite out of his remaining sandwich.

I put my hand on my head in excitement and said, "Well, I have Park Place."

Lavaughn answered, as if nothing had happened, "Well, I have that, too."

I took a couple of long breaths as I quickly analyzed the situation in a half delirium. My thoughts raced, everything from: We gotta send this certified mail; I hope your older brother doesn't steal the piece away from you; to this is your ticket out of poverty! I finally blurted out, "Do you know how much that's worth?"

"Yeah, it's a million bucks," he responded in a matter of fact way, as if he were stretching to put his feet on an ottoman or getting ready to play a lengthy game of bridge.

"Well…?" I paused like, hello, let's go to your house and get it. I said aloud, "I'll help you fill out the paperwork, and I'll help you send it off."

"My mom's not home," he replied.

"You have the key; this is too big to just wait; I'll drive you," I encouraged him.

"Nope, I don't have the key."

"But you always have the key!" I insisted, as I started to sense that I, apparently the most gullible *yehudi* around, was being toyed with.

And after another exchange of questions and Pinocchio answers, I realized that the Boardwalk piece never existed but that Lavaughn had won the game of cerebellum cat and mouse. When I go to McDonald's these days, I'm always reminded of Lavaughn's practical joke, and I can't help chuckling and feeling a little foolish.

Along with the other platoon of kids who came to the gym, Lavaughn and Keith enjoyed weightlifting and bodybuilding. They were gratified to see their bodies grow and become strong. Their self-esteem soared. They liked being able to control who they were and the muscles they were amassing. As the changes became more evident, their friends took notice and wanted to come to the gym, too. After a while, I think most of the kids living in their projects were attending the gym.

During the summer, I decided to enter the kids who trained most consistently in the Junior Olympics in weightlifting. I thought it would be a wonderful experience to load the kids in a van on a scorching August summer day and take them hundreds of miles south out of state to another universe: New Orleans.

When I told the kids we were heading to New Orleans for the Junior Olympics in a month, the look and excitement on their faces was worth half the gold bars locked up in Fort Knox. As soon as I told them, Lavaughn chimed in proudly, "Oh, Louisiana, I know where that's at."

Beforehand, I hadn't imagined how important even a simple trip would be in the kids' lives. But I could tell by the determination shown in their workouts that nothing was going to stop them or get in their way of

Lavaughn puts his energy to good use at a weightlifting meet.

winning.

When we loaded up the van to depart, I was disconcerted to see some of the kids without proper luggage for their clothes. Some held plastic shopping bags. One had an oversized, pre-Cold War suitcase that took up a quarter of the space on the rental van and could have held enough clothes for an extended trip to the Arctic Circle.

We arrived in New Orleans and checked into the hotel, which had been recommended by the host organizing committee. I guess they didn't take into consideration that it was down the block from a couple of strip clubs. I didn't even notice until we walked around the corner in the early evening to eat the famous, touristy Bayou shrimp dinner, and Lavaughn happily pointed to a provocative sign, making sure everyone in our group noticed the blinking neon-lit boobs.

The next morning our troop woke up early after just a few hours of sleep and headed to the competition, eager to show what they had trained for. All the kids did well. They broke their personal records, and almost all received the coveted gold medal. Lavaughn, Keith, and some of the other kids didn't take the medals from around their necks for the remainder of the trip. They were so proud of their accomplishments; you could feel it radiating from their bodies.

After competitions, I felt it was important to explore whatever city we were in so the kids could expand their horizons. Since we were in Bayou country, I thought it would be nice for the kids to take a boat ride and see alligators in their natural habitat instead of at the St. Louis Zoo.

At first, the kids complained that they didn't want to go on a boat ride. They wanted to go swimming instead. I told them that in 10 years they would appreciate having spent a couple of hours learning things about a city different than our own. Although they continued to bitch and moan, once we stepped on the makeshift alligator boat, they enjoyed themselves. The gators snatched up remnants of raw chicken meat from the captain's hooked cane, as we wended our way around the swampy river. I had to hold some of our kids from jumping out of the boat.

For weeks, they bragged to their friends about the wonderful time they had. And every time they had a McChicken, they joked about how quickly the alligators devoured chicken meat.

When we weren't weightlifting, we started a small tennis team. It was basically comprised of Lavaughn, Keith, and Lavaughn's cousin, Lamont. Occasionally we added a couple of other kids, but the need to drive to and from the tennis courts severely restricted the number who could participate. Keith, Lavaughn, and Lamont really enjoyed the special attention they received on our tennis training days.

Lamont in particular had a knack for racquet sports, because his mom and dad brought him along when they played racquetball at one of the city's outside courts. Watching his parents play, he was able to pick up some skills, and he had a great deal of natural talent.

Unlike Lavaughn, Lamont always had this little chip on his shoulder. Though he was a nice kid with good manners, there was always something that was bothering him. He didn't really act like he had an attitude, but it was always written on his face. He was a very smart kid, the kind that when trying, could accomplish a lot; but when he was having a bad day—look out. After a while, I figured out how to deal with it, or so I thought.

We played at least two to three times a week. We tried various courts in the city, some with galvanized fence netting that couldn't be stolen, others with cracks in the asphalt so wide and deep, you might think you were on a hiking trip crossing a big creek. The kids didn't mind the less than ideal

Lavaughn on high school graduation day. *Photo by Carla Scissors-Cohen.*

conditions, even when balls ricocheted out of the cracks, or when the ball hit the wire net and dropped like a pigeon hitting a parked car. Eventually we found a small single court tucked away in a housing project that was rarely used, yet maintained perfectly probably to woo potential new tenants. It turned out to be our little private court. Soon kids and adults would come watch us play on the hot afternoons.

On one particular day, the temperature was well into the high 90s and the infamous St. Louis humidity was registering well beyond Hell. The members of our little tennis club were starting to wither. Since we were training for a small tennis tournament, I tried to push the kids, despite the uncomfortable conditions.

Unfortunately, I started losing it quicker than the kids. Lamont and I were volleying the ball, but he kept hitting it over the surrounding fence. After using up the three balls I was holding, I ran outside the court to gather them and returned for more volleying. Once again, one by one, he smacked them all over the fence. Each time he hit another one over, I raised my voice louder and louder, like a senseless barking dog.

Finally, I ordered him to go get the balls this time. As he went out the gate to collect the balls, I noticed a heavyset woman step off her porch in a lopsided manner and approach Lamont. "You're not going to let that white man talk to you like that, are you? He ain't got no right to talk to you like that!"

Lamont calmly continued to pick up the balls and said softly, "He's not white, he's Jewish." With that he immediately turned his back to her not giving her a chance to respond, and returned to the court to volley some more.

For the next 15 minutes, Lamont didn't hit a single ball over the fence. I quickly realized that he had been intentionally hitting them that way to make me go after the balls since I was closest to the fenced door. Although irritated, to say the least, I must say that I accepted the turn of events as a compliment. By coming back to play and not giving the onlooker any attention or hint of a Louis Farrakhan platform, he was sticking up for me. She eventually retreated inside her apartment.

Over the years, my relationship with Lavaughn and Keith grew stronger. Nonstop, action packed, talkative Lavaughn and the quiet, methodical Keith, turned out to be a couple of the best kids I have ever met and worked with. We shared conversations about everything: life on the streets, how to invest money, Yiddish vocabulary words, like meshuganeh, which Lavaughn had learned from the *Rugrats*. Both were working long hours at Globe and making good money. They excelled in school and were set to graduate and do something positive with their lives.

About a month before their high school graduation, I received a couple of calls from donors interested in donating their old cars. They wanted to know if we could take them for a tax write-off and give them to someone in need. I thought about it for milliseconds and said, "You bet." To the donors such cars were worthless "junkers," but for someone needing transportation, they were magic carpets. I told the donors that I knew two teenagers graduating from high school for whom cars would provide self-sufficiency, not only in traveling to and from a job, but also in commuting to college. With cars, they wouldn't have to limit their college choice to the closest location.

I told Keith and Lavaughn that if they could get insurance, they could have the cars. I have never seen anyone as motivated and as fast as those two when I gave them the news.

After graduation, Lavaughn enrolled in a community college and found a job. Keith found a full-time job, eventually went to a trade school, and secured a job as a drywall hanger. Lavaughn transferred to a vocation-

Keith, another proud high school graduate.

al college and graduated with a computer technology degree.

At Lavaughn's graduation from vocational college, his mother and family gave him a standing ovation as he walked across the stage to get his diploma. I started to tear up, knowing full well that I was witnessing a miracle.

After the ceremony, I went to congratulate Lavaughn. It was priceless to see his mother, stepfather, brother, and grandmother huddled in joy around Lavaughn. His mother stepped out of the huddle and swung around to tell me how much she appreciated everything I had done for him.

"Ya know, Marshall, you were there for the long haul; you never gave up on my son. You helped him make it to this day. My baby graduated from college!" she cheered excitedly.

To this day, Lavaughn and Keith are doing well. Keith left his job as a drywall hanger and is currently working for the police department. He also helped me when I used to renovate houses. One day while we were rehabbing a house, Keith and I were cutting trim and baseboards for the living room. Out of nowhere, he interrupted me while I was sawing a piece of trim and said, "You know Marshall, I'm so glad that the gym was around back then. I don't know what I would have done. It was really bad for me back then. I can't believe I made it out of that place." Then he fell silent.

It's amazing when people decide to share information that perhaps they've been thinking about for a decade or so. Keith continued, "You know, all those trips we went on were real eye openers, even that alligator boat ride. I didn't know what life was like outside the projects."

I smiled and responded, "I've seen a lot of kids come through that place, and I always knew you were going to make it out."

We both hesitantly smiled at each other, as if we were avoiding one of those uncomfortable tearjerker conversations, and continued to manipulate the trim into place.

Lavaughn is working for a communications company in Kansas City and is married with one stepson and a baby boy. During my last visit with Lavaughn in Kansas City, he explained to me that he is very active in his 10-year-old stepson's life and will be for his newborn, too. "Marshall, I'm going to make sure they are successful, there's no doubt about it."

Lamont went into the music business as a rapper. He had a CD come out several years ago with a hot song that was played on the St. Louis radio scene, called "Does Your Chain Hang Low?"

30

The General Cometh

"I need to meet with you about some ideas for how I can help you!" said the unfamiliar voice on the other end of the phone.

"In what way? What do you mean?" I responded.

"I was lying in the hospital in Indianapolis recovering from heart surgery. I wasn't supposed to make it. Then out of nowhere I was reading *Good Housekeeping* and noticed an article about you and your wife and how you were helping inner-city kids with that gym you started. It was a message for me to give back, that I'm supposed to help you," he explained.

"Oh, that's nice," I replied, but I was thinking, are you serious?

"Well, I am here to help you," he continued. "I have some ways I can help you and the kids. I'll be out of the hospital and back in St. Louis next week, and we need to meet." He spoke assertively and without a breath between sentences.

I paused and didn't quite know what to say. Another groisa macher (big dealer), another big talker? I was a gambler, so I decided to take a chance and see who this Dave Stone really was, where this path would lead.

I met him the next week and gave him a tour of the gym. Impressed, he said he was going to raise money for us. I welcomed his fundraising desire and thought it couldn't do any harm, What the heck?

Dave Stone sold used aircraft to small carriers, cargo companies, and the occasional corporate boy looking for a fast toy. He sold them in the United States, small countries in South America, and in various other parts of the world. He was successful in getting financing for buyers who may not have had the greatest credit but needed a plane for their businesses. He was a smart cookie and made a good living.

He was in his early 70s and his health was challenged with a grocery cart full of ailments and heart problems. As he repeatedly told me with a quirky smile, "I'm on my eighth life out of nine lives," but there was no stopping him. His hair was a grayish wave wandering over his skull in different directions, and he hovered in the six-foot-plus category.

When I first met him at the gym for the big tour, I was somewhat surprised by his mode of transportation. I thought that I drove a funkified car, but Dave drove one that was a full step beyond mine. I had imagined that I was top dog at being non-materialistic, but Dave outdid me 10-to-one, as his worn-out tennis shoes attested.

Dave had "Yertle the Turtle syndrome," when there was something he wanted. His pushiness probably shed some light on why he was divorced, but more on why he had a successful business. Sometimes you need the Yertle edge to survive and make it in a crazy business world. I really appreciated that he wanted to roll up his sleeves and sink his hands deep into raising money to help the kids attending the gym.

Within months he raised over $100,000 and didn't really care to be acknowledged for that wonderful feat. Those funds he raised for our programs easily saved many kids from prison, a priceless outcome, the ultimate mitzvah.

One day I noticed in the paper that there was a speaker series coming up at Powell Symphony Hall, a couple of clicks from the gym. There was one speaker among the six in the advertisement who caught my attention, who I thought would be a great role model for the gym kids to meet.

I thought I'd throw this task to Dave. He was unstoppable, no matter the odds. I mentioned that Retired General Colin Powell was coming to town and speaking less than a mile away from the gym. It would be great for the kids to see him, especially since he was contemplating a run for the presidency and had just written a book about his life and how helping out was crucial for our country's future.

Dave instantly said he was all over it and hung up without saying a simple goodbye. I figured this to be a long shot. Powell had just retired from the military. His visibility and stock price were high, but Dave liked uphill battles. Within several minutes, Dave called me back and asked for more specifics, like the date, times, etc. The volley of phone calls went back and forth for the next hour or two.

After a week had passed, and during another meaningless day at Globe, Dave called and excitedly revealed he had been in contact with Powell's secretary, and it seemed that he might be able to come. Within a week, Dave had solidified the entire visit.

When the big day came, we stocked the gym with 20 or so kids and waited patiently for Powell's arrival. You can imagine our anticipation.

When he arrived in the limo that dropped him off, he had just given his motivational speech to several thousand people and had scheduled the visit with us for just prior to his departing flight.

You see famous people like this on the nightly news, and on interview shows like *Meet the Press* and *Face the Nation*, but you don't expect to see someone like that stepping out of a limo in a depressed area with a collapsing bank building dead across the street. Several wine heads, or should I say crack addicts, were sitting at the opposite corner scoping us out, and here this national hero comes stepping out of his limo to see this little gym, and more importantly to meet the kids—it was just plain astronomical.

Powell took his time as he entered the gym and went around shaking all the kids' hands. Some had their jaws on the floor from awe, while others did not understand who it was in front of them. I had little half-pint Michelle give him a tour, and the two hit it off within seconds. They held hands and she showed him the weights, the computers, and our outside garden beds. I found it fascinating that as busy as he was, he made it a point to listen to Michelle. I could see how troops would follow Powell and how he could easily have won the presidency had he chosen to run.

After the tour, he sat down and showed his new book to the kids sitting in a crooked semi-circle around him. He explained how to live an honorable life and, as he put it, "do good things, be a good person." He fielded questions, and one kid innocently asked, "How many people have you killed?" While Dave and I were embarrassed, and some kids laughed, Powell told us that in war, in conflict, you have to do things that might not be what you want to do.

The most compelling thing, though, was when he held up the back of his book and showed us a picture of him as a kid, and then quickly flipped the book to the front picture showing him in uniform as a four-star general. It quickly demonstrated how a child like any of them living in a poor urban area could make it. It put things in perspective for them. Anyone with a dream, a ray of hope, could do phenomenal things in life, if he or she put forth the effort.

We shook hands and Powell told me, while working his way out the metal double-doors, "There is one kid, one of these youngsters that you have here, who will be impacted for life by what you are doing. Remember that."

I smiled back and thanked him for taking the time to visit. As the big visit ended, I was amazed to see that Dave had talked his way into the job of chauffeur back to the airport and had borrowed his friend's Jaguar for the mission.

Years later, Powell made another visit to the gym and to the academy.

Dave Stone helped the gym immensely and then moved on to other projects. He passed away in 2012. We'll always be thankful to him.

Retired General Colin Powell on his first visit to the gym. *Photo by Pamela Wollenberg.*

31

What Comes Around Goes Around

She was at a crossroads: Take one path and clean and jerk a weight she knew she could do and come in third … or the other path, lay it all out and take an uncomfortable chance to successfully lift a weight that would propel her to a solid second.

Her opponent was matching her lifts one by one. Crystal Brown would make a lift and the other girl would answer back with an equal lift. In a national meet like this, it typically comes down to someone choking, making a mistake.

But Crystal was determined. She didn't focus on how she came from a two-bit charity that resembled a south Bronx gym, or how her competitor had the slickest lifting suit at the meet, the latest weightlifting shoes, and coaches who were former decorated lifters with several decades of lifting history. Although I knew it bothered her a little, this wouldn't get her down.

I explained the choices to Crystal with seconds to go. "Lift this and you get a for-sure third, or lift that and you get second, but remember, this will be more than you've ever lifted. It will be a new personal record."

I fought back telling her what to do but hoped that she would go for it. Life is too short to just do the "same old same old," as they say in the 'hood.

"I'll go for it," she said confidently.

Crystal, then 10, small and polite, was one of the many girls who started coming to the gym because their older brothers didn't want to stay home and baby-sit them. As a result, we had just as many girls as boys.

The wave of girls coming with their older brothers was a force to be reckoned with. I don't know if it was growing up in a family of all boys, smack in the middle of the food chain and fending for yourself, or for a kid like Crystal having a God-given talent of rare, sheer strength.

In every contest, Crystal would place in the top three. Eventually, she qualified for the Junior Olympics in weightlifting along with about 30 other boys and girls at Lift For Life. For five months Crystal and the other contenders trained hard to prepare, three times each week for 45 minutes each day.

Crystal knew she was strong but didn't really think that weightlifting was for women, much less girls. Sometimes she just faked that the weight was too hard, and she couldn't lift it, so the boys looking on wouldn't know that she was lifting more than they. Even so, Crystal and the other girls relished the opportunity to travel the country and experience new things.

Crystal's big moment came at the Junior Olympics in Charlotte, North Carolina, where we had 40 of our kids competing. It came after a 12-hour trip in our gym van in which Mr. Lewis, Lawanda, Charles and I took turns driving.

There were six girls in Crystal's weight class. Crystal and four other girls were contenders for the top three places. I predicted that by the end of the day each would be separated by a kilo or two.

Halfway through the competition Crystal was vying for second place with a slight lead because she weighed less than the other girl who was matching her lifts one by one. In weightlifting, a tie-breaker is determined by which lifter weighs the least. From this point on, the rest of the pack had a slim shot of catching her.

Crystal was doing her best ever, but there was that one athlete who was closing in on Crystal, lift after lift. All day long the other athlete's coach was at the scorers' table watching what weight we were going to lift next. He was right over my shoulder like an annoying horsefly at a July picnic. Whatever we picked, he would wait until I walked away and change his athlete's weight to the same Crystal had lifted or to a couple of kilos higher. Slightly annoyed, I tried not to let it bother me, because I knew Crystal was stronger and was going to out lift her, regardless of his strategy.

But things are never perfectly square in this world, and, somehow or other, the communication between the scorers' table and the table where you declare your next lift wasn't working in unison. I gave Crystal my one sentence, two-choice opportunity for her last lift: Do the same thing you can do at the gym, or take a chance and lift this new weight, a new personal record that will bring you in second.

Crystal made the choice to go for it. I immediately told the table with the two volunteers tracking the next lifts what weight we wanted to do. They sent a runner to the scorers' table and made the change in weight to the lifting bar centered on stage.

They called Crystal's name and without hesitation Crystal walked up to the bar and hoisted it over, up to her shoulders, and then quickly above her head—better than a professional Bulgarian weightlifter in the Olympics. As the head judge motioned to put the bar down, all three lights came up white, which signified a good lift.

Crystal smiled and came to me, and we did the ceremonial high-five and gave each other a big hug, while the other girl countered with the same weight. The other girl also handled the weight successfully.

I told Crystal that she'd won second and had broken her personal record. She was naturally excited.

Yet, for some strange reason, because of the confusion between the two tables, some knuckleheaded volunteer accidentally registered Crystal's last lift as a "scratch," or "no lift," and before I knew it, they were handing out awards with Crystal standing on the podium in third place.

I quickly approached the judges' table to complain and explained that she *did* make her last lift, and it was a simple error between the two tables. The judges looked at the results and replied, "Sorry, this is what we have." I told the judges I was going to bring over the other coach who we were competing against, and he would verify the totals. Of course, one would think another certified coach would confirm the correct totals.

Quickly, I went over to the other coach and explained the issue. But he just couldn't remember a thing, even though I distinctly remembered watching him as Crystal made her last lift and seeing his disappointment as he recognized that Crystal had beaten his athlete. I still can't believe that he would let his athlete win on a mistake.

In the end, I guess the injustice ticked me off more than it did Crystal. Coaches are supposed to offer a positive role model, but all that coach did was provide one more example to a bunch of disadvantaged kids that you have to cheat to win. To Crystal, the color of her stamped medal didn't make that much difference. Maybe she was used to settling for whatever she got. So what if she got a cheese burrito instead of a beef one? To some kids, a meal is a meal and much better than no meal at all.

As for me, though, the outcome really stunk. Sometimes, I think I should try letting the current of the river dictate the flow instead of trying to manipulate the course by sticking an oar in it. A Yugoslavian immigrant friend of mine always used to say to me in a thick, sometimes incomprehensible accent, "Marshall, things always work out for the best—you'll learn." But I couldn't let it alone, so it was only after offering a few choice words of advice to the other coach that I congratulated all of our athletes for doing a fine job.

The day after out-of-town competitions, we like to take the kids to the local amusement park as a reward for training hard and doing a good job.

After two days of competition, barely a handful of hours of sleep over the course of the trip, and then a long journey back to St. Louis, why on earth would we take 30 or so kids to an amusement park on a hot day? While I often wondered why we did it, I knew that for one day out of my life, I could endure the amusement parks stenches, dazzling sounds of rides, and the torment of herding kids here and there for the sake of their enjoyment.

After negotiating a discount ticket price for our group, I addressed the battalion at the front gate. We agreed on a rallying point to meet for food. I have learned that it's better to let the kids go off on their merry way and splinter into groups of their own choosing instead of trying to keep them corralled together. Setting specific times to meet for food and ice cream usually works well. They all return at the designated time — bribery perhaps — but hunger is a powerful tool.

There are always some kids who don't like the gravity-defying rides, and for those I become their personal tour guide. It just so happened that this time my tour group was comprised of Crystal and a boy named Dee. Dee was the type of guy who you want to have on your team, a risk taker, but one who knows when not to push too far. He was also a kid who enjoyed games of chance.

I, on the other hand, hate games of chance at amusement parks or carnivals. I never enjoyed throwing a softball at a fake milk bottle, was never strong enough to swing a mallet like Donkey Kong and propel a ball to fly up and ring a bell, and could never shoot a basketball, let alone one barely smaller than the hoop. However, Dee was the man, or at least thought he was.

Toward the end of the day, my aching feet and a suggestion by Dee led me to reach into my pocket and spend several dollars on games to fill up the remaining time at the park. We came across a $2 game that lets you throw three oversized wiffle balls into muffin tins. There were at least 300 muffin holes on which the wiffle ball could land. Most all of them were the stock silver, 20 were painted orange, and one in the middle was painted bright red. Obviously, if your wiffle ball were to land on orange, you'd win a small, stuffed animal; red, you'd win the filet mignon of stuffed animals.

I pulled out $6 and gave it to the attendant while asking myself what the heck I was doing. He handed each of us three balls. Dee, Crystal, and I took turns throwing wiffle balls at the muffin tins.

After a while at amusement parks, especially in August, dehydration sets in and you may start to experience what I call, "Post-Amusement Dysfunction Syndrome" (PADS). The flashing lights, huckster yells, and hot pavement penetrating the soles of your sneakers combine with the scent of fresh vomit mixed with cotton candy, and, if you're not careful, you begin to slowly fade in and out of reality with every heartbeat.

As each of us threw our balls, one at a time, the sound of balls clanking on muffin tin made me become aware that PADS was setting in. The tins we were aiming at were the same ones we had at home. All I could think about was whether my wife was planning to make carrot muffins for Thanksgiving. Focusing on Thanksgiving in hot muggy August was skewed at best. I was definitely losing it.

After Dee and Crystal threw their last balls, I still had one left and began my toss. But right before releasing the ball, I said to myself, "fuck it," and instead handed the ball to Crystal. I guess I must have gotten this from my parents. They always let me have the last "slice," sacrificing their own enjoyment for their kid's pleasure.

Crystal took the ball while looking me in the eyes, and said with a bright smile appreciatively, "Thanks, Marshall!" She threw the ball, and it hit the muffin tins with a resounding kerploink, almost landing without a roll, but then momentum carried it, and the ball rolled and rolled, while we followed it with our eyes like a roulette ball. It rolled in a circle, teasingly missing painted muffin holes and slowly winding down, trickling in and out of every hole it passed until, suddenly it made a big hook and BAM—smack dab in the middle on the single one that was painted red. Los Ultimate!

Crystal's face lit up like a nova.

And, yes, regardless of the PADS that settled in my brain, I jumped up and down shouting gleefully to everyone within hearing distance until Crystal, out of embarrassment, stepped away from me. The attendant smiled as he handed Crystal her oversized, 4x4, plush Winnie-the-Pooh Bear. She hugged it, her arms barely long enough to reach around Pooh's robust belly. As we walked through the park, people turned to look at team "Crystal & Pooh" and smiled. That was her silver medal.

On our long journey home, I glanced back in the rear-view mirror and observed Crystal fast asleep in Pooh's arms.

The next year, during the Junior Olympics, Crystal went against anoth-

er girl with the same first name, same height, and same race. Crystal and the other girl were neck and neck the entire competition, fighting it out for first and second place. The head referee made a mistake, which cost Crystal the gold medal, because he couldn't tell the difference between the two, and before I realized what the problem was, it was too late. Unbelievably, she unfairly lost out two years in a row.

Crystal is currently enrolled in a nursing program and is on her way to becoming the first in her family to graduate college.

Crystal (first row, far right) at an amusement park with other gym members.

32

Mein Kinder

"Are you going to eat all those at once," I asked little Willie Howard.

"Yeah, Marshall, I'm hungry."

It was 8:20, Saturday morning, as I looked at the three shiny Snickers bars clutched in the hands of the 81-pound, 12-year-old. He stood there, huge eyes out of proportion for his small head, looking as if he had arrived from an East African refugee camp.

I wished Willie good luck. "Just do your best," I exhorted, as he left with the other kids from the gym. This time I wouldn't be accompanying them to their weightlifting meet, but instead decided to send two of our other coaches.

Willie wore a large winter parka that swallowed his small frame. Underneath, he was dressed in his 17-year-old brother's worn clothes. Looking after him, I thought, "He is what everyone calls him, 'Little Man.'"

He was a true warrior. He didn't have shit to his name but confidence. Most of us would have folded under Willie's circumstances. His family had been moving from one decrepit apartment or house to the next every couple of months. Still, he continued to make the best of it.

The small room Willie shared with half-a-dozen siblings was covered with ribbons and medals from his countless competitions over the years. He treasured his awards more than we value our bank accounts.

"Little Man" inspired me every time he went on stage for a competition, his expression so serious that I had to restrain myself from laughing for joy. He would walk to the platform, methodically measure his hands on the bar, like a surgeon gauging which scalpel to use, deeply inhale, and then hoist the bar with an assortment of weights that could give most of us a hernia. He was able to lift twice his body weight over his head.

Had I been in Willie's circumstances, I doubt that I could have mustered his determination. I would have fixated on the bed sheet covering my broken bedroom window throughout the frigid winter. Or the fact that my mother never made us kids meals, and I was always, just always, hungry. Would I have realized that my mother's smoking and drinking were probably responsible for my stunted growth? None of this appeared to phase our little warrior, at least while he was on stage.

I often wonder where the paths of my junior weightlifters will lead. It amazes me that here we are in the 21st century, yet a family of seven or eight can still live in an apartment with glassless windows and be using the kitchen stove for heat. We claim we want success for our children. Can we really expect that kids like Willie will grow up with the same bright prospects that other kids have?

Willie's neighborhood reminded me of World War II, when the Nazis bombed London. Some buildings were fine, but others were ripped apart. Across the street from Willie's apartment were buildings leaning like towers of Pisa, a brick or two away from collapsing after a good Jenga game.

Sometimes it seems we're going backwards instead of forwards. In one of Willie's apartments the refrigerator had failed. Fortunately it was winter, so they could keep their few groceries cold by storing them on the porch. My dad used to share stories of how they did that back in the 1930s.

I gave Willie and several others a job at Globe, whether I had work or not. The other kids realized that I sometimes had Willie work more hours than they, although they all needed the money.

Willie never missed a day of coming to the gym. It was a simple choice really: sit at the apartment, hide from thugs on the street, or come down to a free place to hang out. The only issue was those occasions when he had to watch his younger brother and sister. The obvious solution was to bring them along to the gym.

He would bring his sibs one at a time, one week at a time to get me used to having everyone but his mother work out. There was only one minor problem.

It was five in the afternoon on a fall day, and I can remember it vividly. "She's only eight years old," he said softly as he looked sadly into my eyes. I thought for a couple of seconds before responding, and realized she seemed shorter than the miniature poodle I had as a kid. I squinted my eyes at both of them in disbelief, but Willie just looked at me briefly and turned away.

"I don't let young kids come to the gym," I said to Willie, sternly but with some uncertainty. "You know you have to be eight?"

"Megan, tell him how old you are," Willie ordered his sister.

"I'm eight," she said shyly.

"You can stay this once, but you have to be eight," I relented, as I looked at both of them.

A few weeks went by, and lo and behold, the kid keeps coming. Again and again, I would insist that you have to be eight years old to attend, and she would always respond, "But I *am* eight, Marshall."

As the weeks turned into months, Megan became a fixture at the gym. You could tell Megan's clothes were from her older sisters. Her boots looked like they were left over from the Korean War. Her winter coat weighed more than she did, but none of this put sadness in her soul.

Like the other children, Megan enjoyed lifting weights and working out. She enjoyed belonging to a place that cared about her. Every month the gym celebrated the kids' birthdays by providing a birthday cake and presents for each youngster. I'm truly gratified that we have been able to celebrate Megan's eighth birthday with her—two years in a row.

Sibling number three was Lamar, Willie's younger brother and Megan's older one; still another good kid: great manners, very kind, and a desire to stay away from trouble at all costs.

Although he was only nine, Lamar was almost as tall as his older brother, Willie, who was 13. Lamar was appreciative of everything that he got at

Megan (left) and friends on the roller coaster at Six Flags, St. Louis.

the gym, from my spending extra time with him in his workouts to getting an extra plate of barbecue for his quickly growing body.

One day while working out in the gym, I spotted Lamar and couldn't help but notice a terrible odor penetrating my nasal passages. I was hesitant but wanted to verify it was coming from him. I knew that he had to borrow his older brothers' clothes, and usually they were already dirty.

I couldn't take the stench anymore, and for the sake of humanity asked Lamar when he had last bathed.

"A couple of weeks ago; the water is cut off," he replied softly. That is the equivalent of three weeks in kid time. "My goodness!" I countered. I thought to myself, "I can't go 24 hours without a shower, or I'll scream; how can he go for several weeks?"

Driving home after the gym closed, I contemplated how miserable Lamar must feel, especially in school, being taunted for smelling like Pig Pen in "Peanuts." How could he focus at school?

So the next day I called the water company to find out what it would take to reconnect the water. I got word to the mother that I would throw in half, if she would pay the other half. She quickly responded that she was planning to move out of that apartment next month anyway. And not even a thanks for offering to help.

I asked Lamar if he'd like to come to our house to shower and clean up. He replied, "Yes!" quicker than guns being drawn in Clint Eastwood's *The Outlaw Josey Wales* movie. He even called me collect from a corner pay phone the night before to confirm his "health spa" appointment.

He arrived at Globe an hour or so earlier than normal. We went to the gym with the rest of the kids, worked out, and, after Mr. Lewis took everyone home, Lamar stayed with me and we went back to my house. He remembered to bring his clothes in a trash bag to wash them in our washer and dryer.

He went into the bathroom for a while, and when he reappeared dressed and all cleaned up, he had a sparkling aura around him. "Thanks for thinking of me, Marshall."

Now my wife had just paid a house cleaner that day, so my only thought was, "Wait until she sees the bathroom tub!" Water was splashed around the room like a municipal water park, but to Lamar this was his pool party. I knew she wouldn't mind at all.

For now, Lamar's friends would play with him and not shy away or make fun of him. As a result, he could focus on school and just being a regular kid for a few days.

When I dropped Lamar off with the plastic Aldi grocery bag holding his old clothes, he specifically told me to let him out two blocks before his apartment. When I asked why, he answered softly, "I'm gett'n me something at the store." He thanked me as he closed the door with a sheepish smile.

I made a U-turn on the street and noticed in my rear-view mirror that Lamar wasn't walking to the store. "Fooled again!" I told myself, but I understood. He didn't want to be dropped off in front of his apartment because all the other kids from the gym would know something was up. How sad that a child has to take care not to be embarrassed.

THE LONG ROAD HOME

"Marshall," she said in her soft voice. "Do you think you can give me and T a ride to church?" Megan Robinson was standing one late afternoon on the sidewalk in front of her run-down apartment complex, a stone's throw away from the Grand Arts Center.

"Meg, I'm in a hurry to meet Carla and her parents for dinner, and I'm already behind," I answered, while scanning the brightly dressed neighbors loitering on the adjacent steps who were checking out our conversation.

"T" is short for Tira, Megan's sister. They lived on a street densely populated with gang members, the Bloods. Guarding their drug outpost with imperial red shirts, they looked like participants in a Maoist parade. Everyone and their mothers—except Megan and T—wore the traditional Blood red clothes.

"Church is only a few minutes from your house," she wheedled.

Who can turn down 11- and 8-year-olds wanting to go to a children's afternoon Bible Study? "Come on!" a little voice urged inside my addled brain. "Take them to church, a simple oasis and a perfect afternoon escape from this lousy, drug infested neighborhood."

Before I knew it, I opened the door to the two, who eagerly hopped in and buckled their seat belts. "Where is your church again?" This car of mine has been in more adventures in the city of St. Louis than Indiana Jones and the Temple of Doom.

"Oh, it's a couple of minutes from your house. Uh…" she hesitated. "I can't remember the name of the street, but I'll show you. Oh, it's Tabernacle… Tabernacle Church." We drove off, leaving behind the older teenagers with their blunt cigars and overbearing rap music.

"Make a right," Megan said, as we approached Vandeventer and Lindell and passed my favorite fish taco restaurant, now shuttered. "Keep straight," she directed confidently. We continued down Lindell another mile and approached the historic Cathedral Basilica. "It can't be there," I thought to myself.

"Should I turn on Taylor, where a lot of churches are?" I asked.

"Nope, keep straight; I'll show you." We passed the newly rehabbed Chase Park Plaza, and she instructed me to turn left on Kingshighway as she sat comfortably in the front seat.

"This looks right. It's up here!" Megan exclaimed as she studied the landscape of buildings on Kingshighway. But as we crossed over Highway 40 and another mile clicked by on my odometer, we were drifting farther from my house, like a sailboat drifting nowhere fast on a windless sea.

As the minutes passed, I reassured myself that our destination was probably one of the many churches past Interstate 44, which we were now approaching. By now, though, there was no doubt I would be a little late for dinner.

In yoga, when you're doing one of those God-awful contortion stretches with your lower spine, you are taught to take a deep breath. I took a deep breath like that, but still was unable to shake the self-imposed pressure of being late to my in-laws' special anniversary dinner. I glanced in the rear view mirror. T was looking out the car window smiling, eager to make her weekly pilgrimage to the kids' church night. She reminded me of a puppy sticking its head out a car window and getting high from freedom and fresh air. I kept driving.

We traveled south on Kingshighway, the miles rolling by as we continued to move away from my house. One by one, we passed all the pretty churches clustered in the Shaw Botanical Garden neighborhood, yet no end in sight. But I had faith. I believed in Megan and T, even though the "few minutes" by now had turned into thirty.

"Yeah, this is right…this looks familiar. It's up here!" Megan claimed when I asked her for the umpteenth time if we were getting closer.

"Great," I commented tensely, "cause it's starting to get really late."

As bad business deals go south, so did this journey. Finally, I was instructed to turn east on Chippewa. My curls were beginning to get curlier in frustration. I couldn't let Megan and T see that they were being a burden. When we were kids we had an ideal parent or family member to take us places like soccer practice and birthday parties. Those scenarios don't exist for these two city kids. They just had me.

But I was really starting to question this journey. I looked at Megan and asked, "Where are we going? I really need to leave for dinner."

"It's comin' up," she replied in a respectful voice. I guess that's my problem. I believe in these kids. If she says it's coming up, well, by gosh, it's coming up.

"Oh man, what am I doing on my only night off?" I silently asked myself while driving around two kids, one who has believed her church is only a few minutes away for the past 35 minutes, and the other—little T—who has fallen sound asleep in the back seat.

"Go left right here," Megan directed, so we turned onto Jefferson Avenue heading south once more. As my right foot pressed harder and harder on the gas pedal and we passed every single possible church in south city, I simply lost it. It's that tricky feeling you get while waiting for a check in the mail. Every time the mail comes you get excited thinking the check came today, only to be let down that again it hasn't come.

Finally, I said loudly, like a baseball umpire, "Megan, I'm pulling the plug on this mission and taking you guys back home; I just can't do it, just can't."

"Hey, turn here," Megan swiftly interrupted.

"On Highway 44? You gotta be kidding! Farther downtown? Oh geez!" I shouted back as steam came shooting out of my ears.

But before I could make a quick enough decision to take them home, I found myself eastbound on Highway 44 headed towards downtown, too late to make the rational decision to end this trip.

"Go this way," she said while pointing her little finger to the right.

"Highway 55! Oh, Megan!" I exclaimed in disbelief as Highway 44 merged with 55, swinging us away from downtown and deeper south. "I can't believe I accepted this mission," I said to myself.

"We're really close now," Megan reassured me in her friendly voice, while attempting to hide her embarrassment at making me late for dinner.

We pulled off Interstate 55 onto Arsenal, flanking the mega-brewery, Anheuser Busch. I looked up at the big neon sign with the team of stout Clydesdale horses unendingly towing a beer wagon and empathized with the Clydesdales. I was starting to feel like one, carting two kids around the city, going this way and that without a rhyme or reason.

As I made another right or left on yet another street, we approached a church with a large number of kids playing in front. The sign came into focus—Tabernacle Church of God!

Getting my bearings, I suddenly realized that this ride should have taken only ten minutes or less from where Megan and T live. Then I recognized why we had taken the long way around: We had driven the church bus route, the only one they knew.

Megan and T, reenergized like the final fight in Star Wars, jumped out of my car and joined the herd of kids playing on the lawn. "Thanks,

Marsh!" the two shouted in unison and darted off. "See you at the gym tomorrow!" They would take the church bus home.

I began to drive off slowly as a familiar voice came out of nowhere. It was Matt, another kid from the gym, one of only a handful of white kids who come to Lift For Life. "Marshall, what are you doing?" he shouted as I drove off. I looked at myself in the rearview mirror as I shook my head and silently asked, "What *am* I doing?"

THE SHOPPING SPREE

It was summer vacation. That meant no subsidized school lunch program, so it was another Yom Kippur fast for Lamar and his siblings. Lamar's a nice kid. He whines a lot like some kids, but Lamar has an edge on all of us. He has put the equation together and answered it successfully. Lamar explained to me that the reason he "don't do good at school is 'cause there's so much 'stuff' goin' on at home."

I sat in my old fashtunkina chair and thought, *wow, here is a kid who has flunked at least twice but has the savvy to put two and two together.*

Despite the odds, this kid will survive because he knows how. He called me one night to ask if I could move up the day Carla and I planned to take him, Megan and Tira shopping for clothes. I told him I couldn't, even though he was finally graduating sixth grade and needed clothes for his ceremony, a very proud and meaningful day in his first 13 years. But when he called the day before at 9:30 p.m., it broke my heart to tell him we just couldn't, that we would take him as planned.

Luckily, by the power above, his mother took him to a second-hand shop and found some attire for his momentous day. When Carla and I picked the kids up the next afternoon to go shopping, Lamar still had on his clothes that he wore to his graduation. The clothes and shoes didn't quite fit, and looked like they belonged to a medium-height accountant, who just so happened to unload some clothes at a thrift shop for a quick tax write-off. Even so, Lamar was happy with what he was wearing and proud finally to move out of elementary school after being the biggest and oldest kid in his fifth grade class for so long.

As Carla and I pulled up to the apartment from which they would eventually get evicted, the three kids were eagerly waiting on the porch.

As long as I live, I'll never forget that image of the three of them waiting for us. They were just so tired of wearing oversized hand-me-downs from their older siblings and relying on thrift stores. I have nothing against thrift stores, and they serve a good purpose, but what message do kids get when they rely their entire childhood upon thrift store clothes? When they always know that someone else was wearing before what they are wearing now?

So we started on our mission. I was physically tired and had many things I needed to do: fix and clean our house, finish work projects, spend some time doing something just for me on my only night off. I really didn't need to spend money that we didn't have. But I knew that I could freeze whatever was on my agenda momentarily to bring happiness to a few.

We arrived at Target after debating and settling the "who gets to sit in the front seat?" dilemma. Poor kids, rich kids—they're all the same when it comes to positions in cars.

As we walked into the suburban Target, 10-year-old Megan and Lamar stood by my side, while Carla held Tira's hand. The prices were right for a mission like ours, buying mini-wardrobes for three kids who own zilch.

Whenever I think I know it all, I'm just setting myself up for a rude awakening. Carla and I asked the kids what we should get first. I would have guessed sneakers, or perhaps a shirt, but when three kids in unison all exclaim, "Underwear!" at precisely the same time, your heart just wonders what this world is about.

So we picked out some underwear, socks, shirts, pants, and even, yes, jelly shoes. How can you resist a 7-year-old's request for jelly shoes? Something about jelly shoes makes life enjoyable. Of course we made it down the hygiene aisle for toothpaste, new toothbrushes, and deodorant.

I was informed several times throughout our two-hour shopping trip that separate shopping bags were a must. Tira emphasized, "We each need our own bag at the checkout." To T, separate bags meant these were *her* clothes.

We finished off our memorable evening with a meal from Steak 'n Shake. The three kids ate every single crumb off their plates. Either they really didn't know when they would eat again, or they were just plain hungry. That day was very special for all of us. I know it wasn't the solution, but for that moment it helped take the edge off their low self-esteem.

As usual the next day, Lamar arrrived at Globe to do some odd job. He always comes before lunch, go figure. So I sent Lamar to Union Station to get some food. I always tell the kids to hurry because if you don't, it takes forever and when the food gets back the fries generally turn to rubber. Usually they hang out at the arcade for an extra 15 minutes then play at the Disney Store for 40 minutes and by then I'll have binged on enough candy to feed the ants on my block for a month.

Lamar returned with the bags of food for our feast. I went to wash my hands and on my way back I noticed Lamar seated and huddled around the small wobbly table with his can of fruitberry soda pop and his sandwich and fries strategically placed before him. I slowed my pace slightly and watched quietly while Lamar placed his hands together, closed his eyes, and tilted his head up to the sky. This was Lamar thanking God for his 99-cent cheeseburger, fries, and quarter pop. To me it was another miserable and unsatisfying meal. To Lamar it was special. Another meal to get him by until the next one, whenever it might come. His Yom Kippur fast had ended once again, but he didn't have to wait another year like me. How many Yom Kippurs should Lamar endure in a year?

TO READ OR NOT TO READ

Megan enjoyed working at Globe Drug, too. It was the highlight of her week. She loved to make our famous $2 Easter baskets, bag marshmallow crème Halloween pumpkins, fill Christmas stockings, and, best of all, make a few extra bucks so she and T could buy things that her distracted mother wouldn't.

You would think that a child with a bit of cash would run to the toy aisle to buy a doll or some other toy, but she would invest in soap powder to have clean clothes for school, toothpaste, or anything else needed to survive without looking so neglected. Luckily, Globe Drugs was the place to shop. The prices were phenomenal, and a kid making five or ten bucks for a few hours on a Saturday could buy necessities and still have leftover change for a snack or two.

Unlike the other kids that worked there, Megan would use her break time to pull out some crumpled papers from her crammed book bag. At first I didn't notice, but eventually I approached to ask what she was doing.

"I'm trying to do my homework for school," she said.

"Can I help you?" I asked

She smiled and said, "Sure!"

I quickly glanced over the work. It seemed fairly basic given that she was then 11 years old. I sat there for a couple of minutes and watched her stare at the page. I asked her to read it aloud to me, and then I'd give her some pointers on how to complete it.

But when she started, nothing came out of her mouth, not a word. So I suggested she read from a different portion and again only one or two words came out of her mouth. It was clear that she was having trouble reading. How could she function in school let alone life and not be able to read this one page assignment?

In the end, I read the words to her and then helped her do the assignment. I knew that helping her in this one moment would hardly address her problem. It only showed her that I cared.

This was the crazy part: I coached Megan and a host of other kids in bodybuilding and weightlifting, trained them to compete and win numerous awards, turned some into national champions and won national team awards, traveled all over the United States, built up their self-esteem, yet with all that sweat and effort I couldn't help them with the most important thing—their education. They deserved an education!

These were good kids who wanted success but were given the short end of the stick. What type of success can we expect sticking 35 or so at-risk kids in a classroom with an overworked teacher? All they needed was a fishing pole, and they too could be fisherman and be self-sufficient in life. But they were being sent off into the world unable to do a fourth grade assignment or fill out a simple job application.

I am so proud of this country, but there is no word in the dictionary that I can use to say how embarrassed I am that we can send astronauts into space, ship a half million troops to another country, develop laptops computers, cell phones, and the internet, and yet we fail to teach an at-risk 11-year-old girl, a fellow citizen, how to read.

Willie is doing well and working. Lamar moved to Chicago to live with his father. Megan works full time and has three children. Tira is working in the home health care industry.

Lamar, Victoria and me at Six Flags, St. Louis.

33

Do It Now, Because You Can't Do Anything When You Are Dead

One morning in the fall of 1999, I started my daily regimen as usual. I let the dogs out into the fenced yard for a breath of temporary freedom. I filled my lungs briefly as I watched the duo take care of business. Then I proceeded to the front to retrieve the *St. Louis Post-Dispatch*. This week's cereal special at Schnucks was Post Fruity Pebbles, one of the greatest cereals in North America. I poured a generous helping to make sure I had enough sugar and carbohydrates to get me through to lunch, opened the paper, and sat down to dine. As I made my regular scan of the paper, I found a story that more than piqued my interest.

The article was about a new charter school administrator who went to Federal prison for stealing. Charter schools, I would later learn, are free, public schools that operate independently from the school districts they are located in. At the time, only St. Louis and Kansas City were allowed to offer these educational alternatives.

Two competing thoughts bounced around in my head. What the heck is a "charter school"? And if someone who served time could possibly open one, maybe I could open a school. Maybe I finally had a shot at helping Megan learn to read.

I wolfed down my bowl of Fruity Pebbles and hurried off to open the store so I could get down to business: figuring out this charter school thing.

As soon as I got to Globe I called the Missouri Charter School Association to get the scoop on this new type of public school. Although it was 7:30 in the morning, I had to go, go, go. I expected to leave a message but the man quoted in the article, Dave Camden, answered on the first ring. When I identified myself, he said, "I know about you. You started Lift For Life Gym." Turns out Dave had a file of newspaper clippings about the gym. It was as if he'd been waiting for my call. It was "beshert". ("Meant to be" as my rabbi would say.)

I asked him to explain how charter schools work. Dave responded in detail. But I had so much adrenaline flowing I couldn't focus on his answer, other than to hear "a not-for-profit organization could start a school, no problem." BING!

Then I asked, "Do you have to be an educator, or a principal, or a superintendent to open a charter?"

"No, that's the beauty of charter schools. Anyone can start one," he replied.

BING! BING! BING!

Dave offered to help us get started. He made it sound easy, doable. Or maybe I just heard it that way. Either way, I thought if we could open a school, perhaps we could give kids the skills to make it in this world. Maybe we could restack the deck, this time with the cards in their favor. Maybe kids like Megan wouldn't struggle in school and be promoted grade after grade as "special-ed" kids who never learn to read. Maybe kids like Vernon wouldn't skip class and vanish from society, or kids like Raymond would no longer become regular visitors to medium-security "hotels." Maybe Lift For Life could be part of the solution to the urban-education dilemma.

I immediately called Eric Friedman, one of our most enthusiastic board members. If he bought into the charter idea, he could sell it to the rest of the board. He was equally excited about opening a school. He, too, was concerned about the high number of city kids dropping out of school.

Carla was my next victim. I woke her up and treated her to one of my big-picture-but-little-details-we-can-do-this rants. She was hooked.

In life, you have to go for it, because there are no options when you're dead. When you're dead, you're dead.

If you truly believe in something, it will more than likely become reality. As Albert Einstein put it, "Imagination is everything. It is the preview of life's coming attractions."

And after talking with Dave, Eric, and Carla, I was convinced that starting a school could be a reality.

Little did we know that the odds were against us the entire time.

You have to remember, the gym was a little charity that operated donation to donation. We had no endowment, no administrative staff, and no educational experience. Yet what we had was priceless: energy, and lots of it.

And we would need every ounce.

While Kansas City had 16 charters in 1999, the St. Louis charter school landscape was barren thanks in part to the St. Louis Public Schools. SLPS apparently feared a mass exodus of students and threatened to sue any entity who attempted to open a charter school.

See, it's all about the money. School districts are paid per student. A drop in students means a drop in revenue.

"Let 'em sue us!" exclaimed a board member while the group debated expanding into the education industry. He had a point. Our assets at the time included a former garage in a rough part of town, barbells, dumbbells, and a couple of vans. Not really much to sue over. We also figured if we did get sued, the ensuing publicity would only help our cause.

We were cleared for take-off but still needed a few crew members. Our former Ladue High School English teacher Ann Mandelstamm, a long-time gym supporter, joined the team as our educational expert. Solomon helped too, adding charter school development to his coaching duties. And of course our secret weapon, my wife Carla.

Carla left her public relations position at another non-profit and dove full-time into this project. To leave a well-paying job to bring in nothing was, in retrospect, a little crazy. We downsized quite a bit and, frankly, didn't care much about material things. It meant fewer dinner dates and driving our "hoopty" cars a little longer. To us, this golden opportunity to help city kids was worth it.

THE ROAD AHEAD

Each night the gym was full of rambunctious, hormone laden, middle school students. So it made sense to serve that same zany, energetic group during the day. Our decision was sealed when we learned that many students make the decision to drop out of high school as early as sixth grade. As a bonus, Megan could finally get the academic support she desperately needed.

With the board on board, we kicked it into high gear: planning, writing and rewriting our charter proposal until even the non-educators in the group were starting to sound like "educators". Our goal was to open our middle school the following August. It was the equivalent of asking a pregnant elephant with a normal gestation of 21 months to give birth in the standard human nine.

As the charter movement gained steam in St. Louis, I couldn't shake feeling uneasy about a potentially hostile relationship with the St. Louis Public Schools. Many gym kids would still be in traditional public school when we opened our charter and I didn't want to somehow jeopardize their education. It also ticked me off that it seemed the higher-ups at the school district thought we were stealing their students.

So I said "screw it" and called the enemy. Much to my surprise they took my call and invited us downtown for a meeting. Just like that, the superintendent of the St. Louis Public Schools was sitting down with us to discuss helping kids succeed. Turns out little Lift For Life wasn't a threat. With 40,000 students, they could afford to lose sixty "at risk" sixth graders. We offered a solution. We'll take your trouble makers, your underachievers, your most risky at-riskers. Bring 'em on.

I felt better. But we still had a ton of work to do. We were still missing a major puzzle piece – a sponsor.

All the expertly penned proposals and innovative ideas 'didn't mean shit' (as my dad would say) if we didn't have a sponsor. At the time, Missouri law required all charter schools to be sponsored by a public university or the local school district. Our relationship with SLPS had improved but they weren't interested in sponsoring a school. Since Washington University and St. Louis University were private, they weren't an option. And University of Missouri St. Louis (UMSL) was already spoken for.

It was a problem we couldn't fix alone.

Luckily we had Dave Camden in our corner. As part of the Charter Information Center, he was in contact with legislators like Senator Peter Kinder. Now Missouri's Lieutenant Governor, Kinder, is an advocate for school choice: charter, home school, voucher, you name it. He voted for the charter legislation and wanted to see these experimental schools opened in St. Louis. He also happened to represent Cape Girardeau, home to Southeast Missouri State University (SEMO). Officials there would at least listen to our proposal.

Located less than two hours south of St. Louis, Cape Girardeau is a world away from the inner city of St. Louis. We wondered what folks from this small, conservative college town would think of our efforts to help kids from the projects. Would they care that Megan, T and their friends were falling through the cracks and needed a small nurturing environment to succeed in school?

Despite the cultural, political and geographical differences, the folks at SEMO did care. Although the University didn't receive one dime for helping us, they assigned a group of professors and retired superintendents to review our charter.

Would they be supportive of our harebrained scheme to run the school out of the gym the first year? Would they be okay with housing four classrooms in a 5,000-square-foot cinder-block building and using file cabinets, blackboards, and book cases to partition the classrooms? Would it be a problem if each night we rearranged everything so the space could be used for lifting weights and afterschool programs?

The team hit us with a long list of changes and recommendations. At first I thought they were trying to flush us out, to get us to say "uncle" and quit. I later understood that their practical suggestions were designed to make sure we were set up for success.

We were honored and humbled that SEMO president, Dr. Kenneth Dobbins, his team and the Board of Regents took our efforts seriously. Serving as our sponsor would provide the education department a way to expose its students to urban education.

THE MAD DASH

After all the requested changes, SEMO's Board of Regents approved our charter. It was then sent to the Missouri Department of Elementary and Secondary Education (DESE) for final approval. DESE approved the charter in early May. With that, Carla, the board and I did a quick high five and proceeded with the mad dash to open.

The equation was simple. Find 60 sixth graders, hire a principal, four teachers and a social worker; contract food service and transportation; purchase books, supplies and materials; and convert the gym into a school. All within a three-month window. We believed we could do it. So we did it. Nothing could stop us from opening on Monday, August 31, 2000.

Carla, the board, and I began our assault.

First up we needed a principal. Someone who could take my "out of the box ideas" and stuff them into a structure that would become a functioning school. Someone who understood urban middle schoolers. Someone seasoned enough to tackle the challenges, and energetic enough to start a school from scratch. Someone willing to work in a modern day, one-room schoolhouse in a decaying neighborhood.

Someone I wouldn't drive crazy with my endless go, go, go.

Experienced middle school principals were out of our price range and not likely to risk their careers on a new, unproven school. Newly minted administrators didn't have the experience we needed. The other charter schools hired educational management companies to run their schools. We didn't want to go that route.

Instead we worked our contacts.

A board member had a colleague who knew a middle school principal who had recently retired from the St. Louis Public Schools. Was she burnt out? Could we lure her out of retirement? Would she work for peanuts? No, yes, and yes!

Nothing fazed JoAnn Perkins. There wasn't a discipline problem, classroom issue or plumbing malfunction that she hadn't handled in her many years as a principal. JoAnn was a hands-on leader who knew small classes and nurturing teachers were key to student achievement. Free of the bureaucracy of a large school district, she was excited to have the flexibility to teach kids how she knew best. JoAnn recruited teachers, a social worker and a part-time school secretary to round out her staff.

As I worked to renovate the building, Carla orchestrated a marketing frenzy to recruit students. No one was safe from her attack. At Schnucks supermarkets she'd talk to nearly every shopper, regardless of whether they had children. Before long, she had signed up 60 kids from all over the city. Of course, we recruited some gym members, too. Megan was one of them.

OPENING DAY

August 31st arrived and miraculously we were ready. I'll never forget our first day of school. Or the surprised look on our students' faces as they walked into Lift For Life Academy and saw "the ratty old garage" (as the students would call it) for the first time.

They saw orange plastic chairs around folding tables because we couldn't afford desks. They saw bookcases wedged between classrooms because walls were not in the budget. They saw lunchroom tables on the basketball court because there wasn't room for a cafeteria.

They also saw caring, enthusiastic teachers who were ready to do whatever it took to help them succeed.

I'll be forever grateful to the parents of these kids. They too could see beyond the funky building and second-hand furniture. They were willing to take a gamble on Lift For Life because the status quo wasn't working anymore.

Our method was simple; 15 kids in a class, nurturing teachers, and making sure each student knew that failure was not an option.

TRUSTS & SAFE DEPOSITS

Each year over the next three years we added a grade so we'd have a full middle school of sixth, seventh, and eighth graders. We quickly outgrew the gym and purchased the Manufacturers Bank & Trust, a historic bank building in Soulard, a neighborhood south of downtown. We converted the vault into bathrooms and equipped the marble teller stations with computers. It was different but it worked.

Our initial goal was to get the middle-schoolers "caught up" academically and send them back to the better public magnet schools for high school.

It was smooth sailing for a while.

Then the administration at the St. Louis Public Schools changed. Now it was rare for our students to get accepted into magnet schools. After all the hard work helping students like Megan become successful learners, we found ourselves sending them back to the same system that had failed them in the first place.

We heard reports of over-crowding in the classrooms and frequent fights in the halls. Instructors were teaching the same material our students had covered in middle school. Our students were falling through the cracks, again.

It was frustrating. We were powerless. Unless... Katrice Noble, our principal, said it first. "We should start a high school."

REACH A LITTLE HIGHER

It seemed like a natural progression: start with an after-school program, add a middle school then expand to a high school. Except that middle school is often viewed as the "lost years" in education. Students are preoccupied with their changing bodies, exploding emotions and each other. Thank goodness their grades are not part of any permanent record.

High school, by contrast, really counts. Official transcripts and class rankings are an important part of the package. Grades could determine not only where you went to college but if you went at all. High school could set the tone for your entire life. It was not something to fool around with — unless we were serious. And we were. Opening a high school was the real deal. Our students' futures depended on it.

Of course, it wasn't just up to me. We worked again with SEMO to get our ducks in a row and received final approval from the state to add a ninth grade in fall 2008. We were off to the races. We would add a grade each year — topping out at 575 pupils in grades sixth through 12th.

Running a school is a work in progress. We were strategic in our thinking and nimble in our action. If things weren't working, we could instantly make modifications. We offered college prep courses so students would be ready for college and practical classes like driver's education so they would be ready for life. The longer our students are with us, the better their test scores. 89% percent of our seniors graduated in the first graduating class in May 2012. We won't rest until we reach 100%.

Academy students have gone on to SEMO, Truman State, University of Missouri at St. Louis, Forest Park Community College and various trade schools. When Megan and her classmates come back to visit their Lift For Life family it's easy to see their confidence and maturity. I love hearing about their classes and navigating dorm life. I love knowing that our school opened the door to a world beyond the inner city of St. Louis.

On the wall in the lobby reads a sign; Safe Deposits and Trusts. This relic from the building's past is a fitting reminder of our mission. Lift For Life is safe place to build trust and make deposits into the children's futures.

No one, including me, could have predicted that buying a bunch of barbells and benches would have set me on a journey to improve the lives of countless inner city kids. Or, that I would receive far more than I have given.

Opening the gym opened my eyes and my mind. I've learned that friendships can come in all colors, backgrounds and zip codes. I've also learned that no one bats one-thousand. Losing Vernon to the streets was a painful lesson that it is impossible to save every kid. But that doesn't mean you stop trying, or stop caring.

Looking back, I'm still amazed at the resiliency of kids like Megan, Victoria and Cornelius. In many cases, the Gym was the only stabilizing force in their chaotic lives. These kids pulled themselves up, one lift at a time. For my part, I provided a safe place to train. And a crunchy taco every once in a while.

The old bank teller stations made great computer areas for Academy students like Megan.

What's Happening Now

Rough Cuts explores the early days of Lift For Life Gym.

Learn what's new at the Gym: **liftforlifegym.org**

and the Academy: **liftforlifeacademy.org**

Photo by Joe Miller.

Photo by Durb Curlee.

Photo by Suzy Gorman.

About the Author

Marshall Cohen lives in the City of St. Louis with his wife, Carla, daughters Sophie and Trudy Rose, cat Pookins and dog Sparky Pierre. When not busy running Lift For Life he can be found roller skiing in Forest Park, playing table tennis and studying Chinese. He is collaborating with his wife on a children's book about retired racing greyhounds.